The Mexican Peso Crisis

The Mexican Peso Crisis

International Perspectives

edited by

Riordan Roett

LYNNE
RIENNER
PUBLISHERS

BOULDER
LONDON

HG665
.M49
1996

Published in the United States of America in 1996 by
Lynne Rienner Publishers, Inc.
1800 30th Street, Boulder, Colorado 80301

and in the United Kingdom by
Lynne Rienner Publishers, Inc.
3 Henrietta Street, Covent Garden, London WC2E 8LU

Library of Congress Cataloging-in-Publication Data
The Mexican peso crisis : international perspectives
    Includes bibliographical references and index.
    ISBN 1-55587-667-6 (alk. paper)
    1. Devaluation of currency—Mexico. 2. Mexico—Economic
conditions—1994– 3. Mexico—Economic policy—1994– 4. Monetary
policy—Mexico. I. Roett, Riordan, 1938– . II. Program on U.S.-
Mexico Relations (Washington, D.C.).
HG665.M49 1996
332.4'972—dc20   96-8605
                                                        CIP

British Cataloguing-in-Publication Data
A Cataloguing-in-Publication record for this book
is available from the British Library.

Printed and bound in the United States of America

⊗   The paper used in this publication meets the requirements
      of the American National Standard for Permanence of
      Paper for Printed Library Materials Z39.48-1984.

    5 4 3 2 1

Contents

List of Tables and Figures   vii
Foreword, Albert Fishlow   ix
Acknowledgments   xiii

1 International Perspectives on the Mexican Peso Crisis:
  An Introduction
  Clint E. Smith   1

2 The Mexican Peso Crisis and Recession of 1994–1995:
  Preventable Then, Avoidable in the Future?
  Rogelio Ramírez de la O   11

3 The Mexican Devaluation and the U.S. Response:
  Potomac Politics, 1995-Style
  Riordan Roett   33

4 Recent Economic Policy in Brazil Before and After
  the Mexican Peso Crisis
  Celso L. Martone   49

5 The Mexican Peso Crisis and Argentina's Convertibility Plan:
  Monetary Virtue or Monetary Impotence?
  Roberto Bouzas   71

6 Repercussions of the Mexican Monetary Crisis Across the Atlantic:
  Ripples, Breakers, or a Sea Change in European Perspectives?
  Wolf Grabendorff   93

7 Lessons and Conclusions
  Riordan Roett   113

About the Contributors   121
Index   123
About the Book   130

Tables and Figures

Tables

2.1 Paradoxes of Mexican Economic Development:
Positive and Negative Indicators, 1991–1994   12

2.2 Indicators of Reckless Lending by Mexican Commercial
Banks, Selected Years, 1987–1994   14

2.3 Accumulated Percentage Increase in Productivity from 1990
to 1994 in Mexico and Other Selected Countries   20

2.4 Percentage Increase in Exports and GDP of Mexico and
Other Selected Countries Between 1990 and 1994   21

2.5 The Mexican Government's Economic Targets for Calendar
Years 1993–1995 and the Author's Estimates for 1995   25

5.1 The Convertibility Plan in the "Boom" Years:
Indicators of Economic Performance, 1990–1994   74

5.2 The Convertibility Plan in 1995: Adjustment to the
Mexican Crisis   78

Figures

4.1 Brazil's Monthly Exchange Rate Depreciation and Rate of
Inflation, 1989–1995   54

4.2 Monthly Monetary Aggregates: Selected Measures of the
Money Supply in Brazil, 1989–1995   56

4.3 Real Effective Exchange Rate in Brazil, 1989–1995   59

4.4 Brazil's Exports, Imports, and Trade Balance, 1990–1995   60

4.5 Realized Real Interest Rates and Dollar Interest Rates
in Brazil, 1989–1995   62

5.1 Bank Deposits and the "Tequila Effect"   79

Foreword

Albert Fishlow

It is now more than a year since the Mexican 1994 devaluation. The immediate shock was felt by other countries: in the Western Hemisphere, Brazil and Argentina suffered large losses of reserves; in Asia, Thailand and others were affected. But the net consequences of the subsequent substantial decline of the peso and associated retraction of demand have remained primarily a Mexican problem. The so-called tequila effect in the end had little impact. That is one of the remarkable features of this crisis: unlike its historical predecessors it did not simply expand.

One of the reasons, somehow now easily forgotten, was the U.S. response. Although one can criticize the delay and uncertainty, and this book does, the novelty of impressive U.S. commitment clearly was important to this outcome, and adequate assistance to Mexico avoided the potential need for much larger help elsewhere. The U.S. Treasury program, while imposing considerable immediate cost on Mexico (as its significant decline in gross product makes clear), deserves more applause than it has received.

Another important factor was the immediacy of adjustment in capital-importing countries. Argentina, despite a looming election, cut back on demand significantly, to the point where its output growth in 1995 was actually negative. Brazil, with a new president, restrained monetary growth considerably, although allowing the fiscal deficit to increase during the year; the net effects were an inflation rate that had subsided by year-end to about 1 percent a month, and a growth rate that was barely positive in the final quarter. Other countries responded similarly. By the middle of the year, capital imports had begun again.

How can the negative impacts of such an event be still more restrained in the future? Obviously, by not resorting to such policies as late and inadequate devaluation. But the answer goes deeper, as well. It comes down to satisfying the dual requirements for better domestic policy and better international policy.

Mexico in 1994 was not the model of policy perfection it was supposed to have been, as Chapter 2 of this book makes clear. The Salinas government gambled in favor of sharply decelerating inflation and productivity gain to offset overvaluation; and like such predecessors as Chile in 1982, in the end it failed. The current account deficit expanded, and national savings fell. When the money supply grew and interest rates were held down as part of electoral politics—precisely because of possible reaction to Chiapas and political events like the Colosio and Ruiz Massieu assassinations—and U.S. rates rose, reserves dissipated. Much of it, as we now know, was sent abroad by Mexicans. The new Zedillo government, scarcely in office, faced a crisis to which it responded badly. But the more important point is that it would have taken almost impossibly fortunate circumstances to have avoided that denouement.

Everyone now agrees, after the fact, that more current and reliable information is needed to avoid such errors in the future. And Mexico and other countries have hastened to comply. But that downplays the lemminglike quality of international capital flows. They have a tendency to go where they have previously gone, and to stop only when others have stopped. Knowledge ex post will always be inadequate. That is precisely one of the reasons that countries like Argentina and Brazil faced capital flight in the wake of Mexico and rapidly followed restrictive internal policies to forestall the consequences. These are portrayed in this book, but their full effect is yet to be clearly understood.

Something more is evidently needed at the international level to go along with better domestic policy and better knowledge. During the past year, various ideas have surfaced. One thing that is clear from the difficulties of the Mexican rescue is that the United States cannot be relied on to provide substantial resources for other countries. A relatively easy answer is that the International Monetary Fund (IMF) General Agreements to Borrow should be doubled, as agreed at the June 1995 summit of the Group of Seven. But that answer is a little deceptive: to use the increased funds, a letter of intent is necessary. And that usually takes longer than the days, or even hours, that the markets can wait.

Another possibility is a special IMF matching-fund facility that would be self-financing and automatically disbursing. A country with large capital inflows would be encouraged to make special deposits with the IMF. In return it would be entitled to withdraw some multiple of its initial quota. A major virtue of such an arrangement is that it would avoid the need for governments to approve an increase in IMF quotas. But there remains the danger that a small number of debtor countries might, in the pressure to be first to exert their claims, set off a run that would quickly deprive the fund of resources.

Yet another way to avoid the problem of the significant domestic consequences of sudden capital outflow is to use tax-like devices to limit inflows. Such restrictions have appeared in recent years. One of the countries that has used them most effectively is Chile. A consequence has been not only lesser capital flows, but flows more allocated to direct foreign investment than to accumulation of financial assets. The broad reading, across the variety of national experiences, is that such devices can work. But obviously the more they are relied upon, the less effective they will be.

There is still another solution, but that comes after the fact. Various schemes have promoted the feasibility of international bankruptcy. To the extent that the purpose of bankruptcy procedures is to provide a standstill on payments outward, countries already have that option—and have used it. Attempts to create an international bankruptcy court face serious difficulties. Such a court would not possess the power to seize collateral, nor would it "replace" the government of a country the way that a new management is created for a reorganized firm.

In the end, there may be no practical universal solution. But if we are to learn positively from the Mexican experience, there are marginal, but effective, ways to encourage compensating adjustments during periods of capital inflow and so avoid the catastrophe of that example.

The authors of this book provide a very useful account of the Mexican case, as seen internally and externally in neighboring countries, lenders as well as borrowers. That perspective is essential if we are to avoid similar crises. Careful reading of the book will benefit those concerned with both domestic and international policy.

Albert Fishlow
Senior Fellow for Economics
Council on Foreign Relations, New York

Acknowledgments

This book, a special publication of the Paul H. Nitze School of Advanced International Studies (SAIS) Program on U.S.-Mexico Relations, was completed through the committed effort of various individuals, to whom I extend my sincere gratitude. I would like to thank my fellow authors for their insightful contributions; Guadalupe Paz, the program's coordinator, for managing all the details involved in the editing and publication process; and Wendy Campbell for her excellent editing work.

Finally, I would like to acknowledge that the support of the William and Flora Hewlett Foundation has been essential in allowing the program to contribute such works to the field of U.S.-Mexico relations.

Riordan Roett

1

International Perspectives on the Mexican Peso Crisis: An Introduction

Clint E. Smith

This book provides one of the first opportunities to examine international perspectives on the Mexican financial and institutional crisis of 1994 and 1995. The purpose of the book is to offer a wide range of views on the crisis from Argentina, Brazil, the United States, Europe, and Mexico itself. The authors were asked to raise critical questions and issues related to the current Mexican scene rather than to seek, particularly at this early date, any definitive answers. In this spirit, they have addressed such questions as: What could Mexico have done to prevent the December 1994 crisis? Is the most recent economic program of the administration of President Ernesto Zedillo adequate to meet the nation's critical need for stability and institutional reform? How well did the Clinton administration and the U.S. Congress respond in their efforts to support Mexico after the crisis erupted? What are the long-range implications of recent events in Mexico for the economies and economic plans of Argentina, Brazil, Latin America as a whole, and Europe? What is an appropriate role for the European Union (EU) in Latin America?

It will be recalled that the administration of Ernesto Zedillo got off to an auspicious start on December 1, 1994. After his resounding, and convincingly genuine, electoral victory in August 1994 over rival candidates of the right and left, the young president inaugurated his administration with a well-received address and a new cabinet that included as secretary of finance Jaime Serra Puche, whose work as secretary of trade and industry in the successful negotiation of the North American Free Trade Agreement (NAFTA) had earned him a favorable reputation in international trade and financial circles.

The first weeks of the Zedillo presidency were almost triumphalist in nature, with the promise of early institutional reforms and the December 8 prediction by Serra Puche that in the coming year Mexico would enjoy real gross domestic product (GDP) growth of 4 percent and an inflation rate of 5 percent. Questions about the wisdom of Mexico's international

1

financial policies were dismissed, and the door was kept closed on any discussion of a possible devaluation: "The exchange rate policy will maintain
the established flotation band, which gives the financial authorities a maneuvering margin to confront transitory problems," Serra Puche said.[1]

Only twelve days later, on December 20, 1994, Mexico devalued the
peso, initially by attempting to expand the "flotation band" by 15 percent.
The controversial management of this unexpected move (which went
against the advice of many international investment analysts) exacerbated
investor fears and would shortly result in a further, uncontrolled fall in the
peso after Serra Puche announced that the peso would be allowed to trade
freely against the dollar. "The financial authorities," he explained, "have
decided that supply and demand will freely determine the rate of exchange
until the currency markets show conditions of stability."[2]

The finance minister's subsequent trip to New York did nothing to reassure foreign investors. In the face of a deepening crisis, President
Zedillo announced on December 29 Serra Puche's replacement by Guillermo Ortiz, a former undersecretary of finance who was then serving as
secretary of telecommunications. But the promised prompt unveiling of an
emergency plan to confront the economic crisis was slow in coming, and
by that time the peso had lost 50 percent of its value. By early January the
crisis had reached its nadir.

The contributors to this book, as outlined below, take the Mexican crisis from it earliest stages and seek not only to describe the events that took
place between late 1994 and early 1996, but also to comment on the Mexican scene from their particular and often quite different perspectives.

A Mexican Perspective on the Crisis

Rogelio Ramírez de la O, a respected, independent economic analyst in
Mexico City, addresses the monetary crisis in a wide range of its aspects.
Ramírez points to what he views as the seriously flawed macroeconomic
policy and strategies of Zedillo's predecessor, Carlos Salinas de Gortari,
and discusses both the failure of the Salinas administration (1988–1994) to
recognize and carry out an orderly devaluation during the course of 1994
and Zedillo's own mishandling of the economic situation at the outset of
his presidency in December. He also examines perceptions in Mexico of
U.S. executive and legislative branch reactions to the crisis, and what
those perceptions portend for the future of Mexican-U.S. relations. His
analysis points to four critical misperceptions left over from the misguided
economic policies of the Salinas administration: that a large current-
account deficit is self-adjusting and should not be a concern of the government; that productivity growth would offset the appreciation of the
peso in real terms; that Mexico could carry large external deficits for a

long period of time without suffering serious consequences; and that the goal of privatizing state entities should be to maximize initial revenues.

On the subject of U.S. support to Mexico during the crisis, Ramírez notes that as part of the bilateral Exchange Stabilization Fund (ESF) agreement, Washington is now involved in monitoring Mexican economic policy—a situation the author views as fraught with political risk. He advises the United States to disengage itself at the earliest possible moment and turn any such monitoring over to international financial institutions such as the International Monetary Fund (IMF), insofar as that is possible at a time when the old economic paradigms, and the institutions themselves, are in question.

Finally, he notes that the long-term consequences of the crisis will touch every sector of the Mexican populace. He looks to a new generation of Mexican entrepreneurs to emerge and take the lead in the next recovery of the economy, and he calls for the government to ease foreign investment laws and regulations and to actively encourage foreign investors and financial institutions to bring to Mexico the fresh resources it requires for such a recovery to begin.

The U.S. Response and Potomac Politics

From the initial moments of the crisis, two parallel actors were front and center: the Mexicans, in their effort to manage the emerging crisis, and the Clinton administration, which was dominated by the dual fears of instability in the international financial system and domestic political fallout from attempts to provide Mexico with clearly needed support.

In the opening sections of his chapter, Riordan Roett, an expert on Mexico based in Washington, D.C., covers the origins of the Mexican crisis, the deteriorating financial situation in Mexico, the series of Clinton administration responses to the need to support the Mexican government that after false starts resulted in the ESF package, and the emerging opposition to the Clinton efforts. Roett makes note of the strange bedfellows who gathered in opposition, ranging from the freshman Democrat from California, Senator Barbara Boxer, to veteran conservative Jesse Helms (R.-N.C.) and goes on to analyze the sharp and at times acrimonious debate that ensued, including attacks on NAFTA, Wall Street (supposedly a major beneficiary of the so-called bailout), and Mexico itself.

Roett makes the interesting point that the White House did not take long to play what has over recent decades been a trump card in Washington politics: the national security issue. By raising the specter of potential instability in Mexico, with which the United States shares a 2,000-mile border—and indeed throughout the Western Hemisphere—if support for Mexico was not forthcoming, the Clinton administration was in effect calling on Congress and other critics to acknowledge the leadership role that the U.S. presidency has played—certainly over the past six decades—in international security.

But the new Republican Congress emphatically rejected those assertions, which surely raises an important question: Was the failure on Clinton's part merely a reflection of his weak leadership, or does it portend some historic sea change in the balance of power between the executive and legislative branches in a post–Cold War future? Roett concludes that it now appears highly unlikely that much progress can be made in the near future on pressing trade, financial, or other bilateral issues that are in fact of great significance to the national interests of both Mexico and the United States.

Brazilian Interpretations and Policy Responses

The Mexican economic crisis is being interpreted in Brazil as policy failure, as a possible premature end of an unsustainable credit cycle, and as a potential breakdown of the neoliberal development model so popular in the early 1990s in Mexico and elsewhere in Latin America. In Chapter 4, Celso L. Martone, an economist at the University of São Paulo, explores all three of these not necessarily mutually exclusive perspectives.

Martone views the Mexican crisis as compelling evidence against the exchange rate–based stabilization model, which in essence links domestic and world price levels by linking nominal exchange rates. He argues that pegging the exchange rate "is neither necessary nor sufficient for monetary stability," adding that permanent stability will require among other things a balanced budget, a consistent central bank monetary rule, and strong public confidence. Martone also observes, in Brazil and elsewhere, a kind of "neodependency" interpretation, which stresses the dependency of Latin American economies on the international (and particularly the U.S.) credit cycle. Adherents of this argument note that the Latin American debt accumulation in the 1990s is not all that different from the previous cycle in the 1970s and the crisis of 1982, and that a decade was required for recovery from that disaster.

Martone presents a thorough analysis of recent economic developments in Brazil, with a focus on the 1989–1994 period, including the failure of the Collor Plan in 1991–1992 and the premature collapse of the Collor regime in September 1992, which resulted primarily from the discovery of a pervasive pattern of corruption. The Collor failure retarded structural reforms in Brazil, inflation returned to the four-digit levels of the past, and GDP and industrial output fell precipitously. But it must also be recognized, Martone points out, that Collor did succeed in promoting trade liberalization, initiating privatization, and calling the financial world's attention to Brazil as an emerging market.

The Itamar Franco administration that succeeded Collor had no clear economic policy articulation. It did maintain trade liberalization and privatization, but it also promoted dramatic fiscal expansion, with federal expenditures leaping 70 percent in real terms in 1993/94, much of that in government salaries. Despite high inflation, real GDP actually grew 10 percent in 1993, fed in part by federal expenditures, a new inflow of foreign capital, and rising exports to a more robust world economy. Nevertheless, there was growing recognition that a new stabilization plan was needed. That became the responsibility of Fernando Henrique Cardoso when he became minister of finance in May 1993, taking with him to the ministry a skilled team of economists from his Brazilian Social Democratic Party (PSDB).

The new stabilization plan was launched in February 1994, and its success became a launching pad for Cardoso's successful campaign for the presidency; he was elected in October 1994 and took office on January 1, 1995. His current tasks, Martone points out, are to keep inflation at an acceptable level (perhaps around 30 percent) and to bring the current-account deficit down to the 2.0 to 2.5 percent range. In the longer term, Brazil needs institutional reforms in fiscal policy and tax collection; greater private sector participation in such sensitive industries as electric energy, petroleum, and telecommunications; and, perhaps most important, reform of the electoral and political party systems.

Martone concludes by noting that the timing of the Mexican crisis of December 1994 was particularly difficult for Brazil since it came just as the new administration was taking power. The crisis appears to have provoked a shift in government priorities toward seeking balance-of-payments equilibrium at a time when international capital markets were contracting because of the uncertainty of the Mexican situation. Unfortunately, Martone notes, Brazil's recent move toward free trade has been a casualty of this shift in priorities. Under the guise of a "new industrial policy" the government is reinstituting trade barriers to reduce the current-account deficit and improve the balance of payments.

An Argentine Perspective

The economic policies of the Carlos Menem administration in Argentina have attracted considerable interest, especially since the launching of the Convertibility Plan in 1991. In general, Argentina has enjoyed a period of rapid economic growth and falling inflation rates during most of this time, but the international financial environment, particularly the recent rise in

U.S. interest rates, has halted the expansionary trends in Argentina, and the country now finds itself threatened with a recession. In his chapter, Roberto Bouzas, an economist writing from Buenos Aires, analyzes the history of the Convertibility Plan and the impact of international trends, including the Mexican crisis, on the Argentine economy over the past year or so. The first section of his essay offers an overview of the plan prior to the Mexican crisis, while later sections examine how the Menem government has reacted to the Mexican crisis and what Argentina's economic prospects are in the near to midterm.

To the surprise of many international observers, the Menem regime, which came to power in mid-1989, undertook a sweeping structural reform program consisting of extensive privatization, deregulation, and a dramatic liberalization of trade and financial services. That was followed in April 1991 by the new Convertibility Plan, whose principal tool was ensuring the full convertibility of the Argentine currency into U.S. dollars; the exchange rate was backed by the central bank, which was thus inhibited from deficit financing through currency issuance, with the top priority being fiscal adjustment. Bouzas illustrates remarkable achievements associated with the plan, including rapid real GDP growth, rising investment, and plummeting annual inflation rates, which dropped from 4,900 percent in 1989 to just over 3 percent in 1994.

Argentina's domestic economic performance was not matched, however, in the external sector. During the early 1990s, Argentina has suffered a steady deterioration in its trade and current-account balances. The trade balance fell from a U.S.$8.3 billion surplus in 1990 to a $5.8 billion deficit in 1994, due mainly to a fivefold increase in imports and only a marginal improvement in exports. Inflows of external capital were so robust, however, that despite the trade imbalance, the reserves of the central bank actually rose from $4.8 billion in 1989 to more than $16 billion in 1994. Nevertheless, as Bouzas warns, this situation is inherently unstable, as demonstrated by the decline in foreign capital inflows resulting from such exogenous factors in 1994 as rising U.S. interest rates and, of course, the Mexican crisis.

In fact, crisis management became the dominant theme in Argentine economic policy management after the events in Mexico at the end of 1994. Bouzas explains that in five short months capital flight caused the central bank's reserves to fall from $16 billion to $11 billion by May 1995. The situation was complicated by an active presidential campaign, leading to May elections. Menem won handily, gaining 50 percent of the popular vote against his opponents.

Bouzas concludes by asking whether in the present circumstances the rigid Convertibility Plan is a viable policy choice. He observes a growing sense in Argentina that this rigidity is impeding a long-term push toward robust and sustainable economic growth and that changes in the country's macroeconomic strategy will therefore be necessary.

European Perspectives on the Crisis

Some European observers who followed events in Mexico during the first half of the 1990s were as aware as some of their U.S. and Latin American colleagues of the need for a change in the course of Mexican economic policy management. From a European perspective, a decision to devalue the peso would not have seemed bizarre—after all, the lira, peseta, and pound had undergone painful devaluations during the same period. Indeed, and despite the initial mishandling of the devaluation, Wolf Grabendorff, who is a close observer of Latin America from his vantage point in Europe, concludes that the financial repercussions of the early stages of the crisis are now largely under control.

He also points out that the EU view of the Mexican crisis was from the beginning more sanguine than that of the United States. In fact, some EU member states expressed anger over U.S. pressure to support the international rescue package for Mexico. As Grabendorff observes, "Lingering EU objections concern both the package itself and its presentation as a fait accompli" on the part of Washington. That attitude was due in part to the EU notion that even large losses by financial institutions holding Mexican bonds did not pose a serious threat to the global financial community. Moreover, Grabendorff writes, "the massive rescue plan posed a 'moral hazard' that might encourage precisely the kind of behavior that *would* launch a systemic crisis . . . a sure way to render the world financial system fragile indeed."

Grabendorff also examines what he describes as a changing U.S. trade strategy toward the Western Hemisphere. Essentially, this consists of a greater wariness in pursuing broader free-trade initiatives, particularly on the part of the U.S. Congress, on both the Democratic and Republican sides of the House and Senate. As a result, he sees little prospect of any expansion of NAFTA before the next century.

Grabendorff also presents a distinctive European perspective on what he describes as "Washington's much more aggressive and coherent strategy to raise the U.S. profile in Latin American markets," a goal he identifies until late 1995 with U.S. undersecretary of commerce Jeffrey Garten. "The Garten strategy," Grabendorff says, "involves the use of a wide range of tools to promote inter-American commerce: cabinet-level business development missions, specific target contracts selected by trade officials, pressures by diplomatic delegations abroad, credits from federal financial agencies, . . . the threat of retaliatory action, . . . and new export assistance

centers to help small and medium-sized U.S. enterprises." It is interesting
to note that what Grabendorff implicitly criticizes as a "more aggressive"
new U.S. trade posture is in fact remarkably similar to trade strategies that
have been pursued by many major EU members over several decades!

Grabendorff includes a very useful analysis of the Mexican crisis,
with its unfavorable impact on the U.S. economy and on prospects for expanding NAFTA. He concludes that more salience might now be given to
Mercosur and other regional South American trade arrangements. He concludes that the EU might seek to ensure that international financial institutions pay greater attention to regional interests and that EU analysts believe that the Mexican crisis "has demonstrated beyond a doubt the
superiority of regional *integration schemes* (which Europe and Latin
America favor) over mere *free-trade areas* (which the United States has
advocated)." Thus, he believes Europe is more in tune with Latin American needs and aspirations than the United States.

Summary

The authors of the chapters in this book have provided a broad range of international perspectives on recent developments in Mexico, with a focus
on the economic crisis of December 1994 and the efforts of the new administration of President Zedillo to cope with a series of economic, political, and institutional challenges. A clear picture of the depth of the crisis
emerges from the authors' explication of the policy errors of the Salinas
administration that precipitated the crisis, as well as the early mishandling
of an admittedly difficult situation in the first weeks of the Zedillo administration. Fortunately, financial indicators at the conclusion of Zedillo's
first eighteen months in office suggest that Zedillo's team has ultimately
learned at least to cope with the economic situation; by mid-1996 basic—
but not yet solid—financial stability appeared to have been achieved.

There is little doubt that the financial crisis was greatly ameliorated by
the intense efforts of the Clinton administration to come to Mexico's assistance. After some false starts, the assistance package grounded in the
Exchange Stabilization Fund agreement was an essential element in defus-
ing the *tesobono* time bomb and in giving the Mexican government the
economic policy space it needed to take other necessary measures.[3] European criticism reported in this book of the U.S. action should surely be
tempered by the obvious need for early assistance after the December 1994
crisis flared. Although it is hard to judge what the impact on other Latin
American countries would have been without firm and effective U.S. action, the proposition that the likely negative impact of the crisis on such
countries as Argentina and Brazil was ameliorated by the ESF agreement
is not a difficult one to accept.

This is not to say that the Mexican crisis was optimally handled from its inception—far from it. Serious initial mistakes, covered in some detail by several of the authors, marked the early days of the Zedillo government, and certainly President Clinton lost a lot of momentum in his early, failed efforts to achieve a bipartisan solution with his Republican-led colleagues in the U.S. Congress. The difficulties both Mexico City and Washington had in addressing the crisis in fact offer valuable lessons for efforts to identify viable new alternatives to international financial crisis resolution. One such alternative is to expand the role of the IMF to give it greater authority to act as a lender of last resort, a suggestion proposed by Canada at the June 1995 meeting of the Group of Seven in Halifax. Details of that proposal need to be worked out, but it would appear to offer advantages over the ad hoc rescue operations usually launched in cases such as the Mexican one.

Finally, it would be unwise to breathe too deep a sigh of relief at the current easing of Mexico's financial situation. The nation still faces serious economic problems—in faltering production, burgeoning unemployment, a weakened internal banking system, and a decline in public confidence in the regime, which has not as yet been mitigated by efforts of the Zedillo government to institute essential, basic reforms of Mexico's legal, political, and social institutions. Fortunately, there appears to be a healthy recognition on the part of Mexicans of all political parties and ideologies that those institutional reforms in the coming years are essential to Mexico's continued stability and prospects for renewed, sustainable economic growth and development.

Notes

1. Reuters, December 9, 1994.
2. Reuters, December 21, 1994.
3. *Tesobonos* are short-term dollar-denominated bonds that were coming due when the crisis began in December 1994.

2

The Mexican Peso Crisis and Recession of 1994–1995: Preventable Then, Avoidable in the Future?

Rogelio Ramírez de la O

On December 19, 1995, the Mexican government lifted the upper limit of the band in which the peso was traded against the dollar by 15 percent, in effect signaling a devaluation. That was the public's interpretation, despite assurances by the new finance secretary, Jaime Serra Puche, that widening the exchange rate band was intended only to provide the monetary authorities with flexibility in managing the peso as the Zapatista uprising in Chiapas dragged on toward its second year.

Events proved Serra Puche's protestations simplistic in the extreme. A sharp peso devaluation followed, accompanied by a debt-payments crisis. The newly inaugurated administration of Ernesto Zedillo Ponce de León was helpless to convince the markets and the international community that it could control a difficult albeit not abnormal financial situation. Since the principal qualifications touted by the Zedillo team during the presidential campaign of 1994 had been its capacity to handle economic problems, the peso problem inflicted severe damage on the team's credibility, damage from which it has not yet recovered. When the president admitted on March 14, 1995, to the *New York Times* that "a few days after we devalued, I became convinced that we did not have a current-account adjustment problem," a palpable suspicion among the populace was confirmed: the new administration did not fully grasp the complexities of Mexico's economic situation.[1]

This chapter discusses the peso crisis in the broader context of the flawed macroeconomic policies and strategies Mexico pursued during the early 1990s. The first section reviews those recent pursuits in an attempt to show that the devaluation was not only foreseeable but also inevitable by the end of 1994. The second section details the features and implications of the economic adjustment program instituted after the devaluation. The third section describes Mexicans' perceptions of the U.S. rescue package and speculates on some long-run implications of the crisis.

Macroeconomic Policies and Progress in the Early 1990s:
What Would Have Prevented the Peso Crisis?

Mexico successfully controlled inflation in the early 1990s with an orthodox strategy that included eliminating the fiscal deficit, liberalizing trade,
and establishing monetary restraints. Together those policies resulted in an
annual inflation rate of 8 percent in December 1993, when the North
American Free Trade Agreement (NAFTA) with Canada and the United
States was about to go into effect.

Other macroeconomic indicators, however, showed a paradoxical situation. Table 2.1 illustrates how huge foreign capital inflows not only
failed to generate expanding economic growth but also necessitated a rising ex ante interest rate, despite the falling inflation. A similar context
across the Atlantic had caused some European countries to abandon the
European exchange rate mechanism (ERM) in the autumn of 1992; exchange rate stability had come to depend on reducing economic growth as
speculative pressures could be contained only with tight macroeconomic
policies.

That was not, however, the policy response in Mexico. First, it took a
long time after economic growth decelerated for the Mexican government
to admit to the fact. In the autumn of 1993, for example, Pedro Aspe, then
finance secretary, provoked a public outcry when he referred to the notion
that wages were low and unemployment high as "a perfect myth." Earlier,
when the second quarter of 1993 posted zero growth, the government had

**Table 2.1   Paradoxes of Mexican Economic Development: Positive and Negative
Indicators, 1991–1994**

	1991	1992	1993	1994
Positive Signs				
1. Public sector balance (% of GDP)	–0.5	1.6	0.3	–4.0[a]
Consumer inflation (Dec.–Dec. %)	18.8	11.9	8.0	7.0
Total foreign capital inflows (U.S.$ billions)[b]	23.0	25.6	29.4	9.9
2. Foreign direct investment only (U.S.$ billions)	4.8	4.4	4.4	8.0
Negative Signs				
Annual growth in GDP (%)	3.6	2.8	0.6	3.5
Ex ante interest rate, Cetes 28-day average (%)	4.8	6.4	8.4	–13.2[c]
Current-account balance (U.S.$ billions)	–14.9	–24.8	–23.4	–28.9

Source: Bank of Mexico, *Indicadores Económicos* (Mexico City: Bank of Mexico, June
1995).

[a]Includes financial intermediation, namely, credit subsidies from development banks.

[b]Includes foreign direct investment and portfolio investment, as well as "errors and
omissions."

[c]Average rate over expected annual inflation of 35 percent in 1995.

contended it merely reflected a healthy economic adjustment, as inefficient producers were being eliminated by a more competitive economy, while the efficient ones continued to perform. Increasing anecdotal evidence of a widening recession, however, began to convince other members of President Carlos Salinas de Gortari's cabinet that growth was being sacrificed to the objective of low inflation when, in fact, behind the government's rhetoric of maintaining inflation low, the ultimate objective was to maintain the peso within a narrow nominal exchange rate. Growing criticism within the cabinet caused the first fissures to appear in an otherwise united team, another indicator of exchange rate risks. That is, when a government pursues a nominal exchange rate at the cost of sacrificing economic growth and at the same time not everyone in the cabinet is convinced that it is the appropriate strategy, a devaluation risk emerges. This is because opposition to the exchange rate policy may grow within the government and become evident to market players.

Aspe has since confirmed the fissures. In mid-1995, he noted that in November 1994 a group led by then president-elect Zedillo asked President Salinas to devalue the peso. The discussion divided the participants at the meeting into two groups: "those who wanted an immediate implementation [of the devaluation] at a floating regime, and those who argued for a restrictive monetary policy to significantly raise interest rates and the rejection of an exchange rate devaluation."[2]

There was some truth to the protestations of the finance ministry and the Bank of Mexico that the restructuring of Mexican industry was forcing some producers out. The more fundamental fact, however, was that macroeconomic distortions, such as high interest rates and a strong peso, had brought about great difficulties for domestic industry. Those distortions were responsible in part for the flood of bank credit for consumer spending in 1993 and 1994.

As shown in Table 2.2, commercial bank lending for consumption grew in real terms by 457.7 percent over the period 1987–1994, while that for housing grew 966.4 percent. By contrast, lending for the manufacturing industry grew by 130.6 percent and total bank lending by 107.7 percent. That credit boom explains much of the widening deficit on the external current account, which must be attributed to a fundamental misallocation of resources and not a continuous rise in investment, as the government alleged. That misallocation, in turn, explains why commercial banks' balances had begun to deteriorate long before the devaluation, as growth in real wages, also shown in Table 2.2, was slow. Since unemployment was rising during this period of adjustment, the "increased market" for consumer borrowing mirrored a high, unsustainable appreciation of the peso exchange rate. Enthusiastic and reckless bankers, too anxious to recoup the high prices paid for Mexico's reprivatized institutions, were set to crash with the first shift in the business cycle.

Table 2.2 **Indicators of Reckless Lending by Mexican Commercial Banks, Selected Years, 1987–1994 (in billions of 1994 pesos)**

	1987	1990	1993	1994	Real Increase 87–94 (%)
Real-wages index (1987=100), adjusted for productivity	100.0	103.6	104.8	102.6	2.6
Total outstanding bank loans (1987 NPs)	420.004	382.843	624.699	872.300	107.7
For manufacturing industry	52.954	67.190	90.145	122.100	130.6
Housing	10.156	19.988	82.437	108.300	966.4
Social	10.156	19.988	28.906	37.100	265.3
Medium	0.000	0.000	24.303	37.000	
Other	0.000	0.000	29.228	34.200	
Consumption	7.979	27.983	44.644	44.500	457.7
Credit cards	0.000	0.000	31.583	31.200	
Durable consumer goods	0.000	0.000	13.061	13.300	
Housing + consumption	18.135	47.971	127.081	152.800	742.6
Credit for trade, retail, wholesale	21.036	49.047	92.822	128.900	512.7
Average real peso exchange rate (NPs per U.S.$ = 1.000)	1.000	0.710	0.583	0.594	−40.6

Source: Bank of Mexico, *Indicadores Económicos* (Mexico City: Bank of Mexico, various years).

Short-Term Management of Currency Pressures

Since early 1993, the Salinas administration had been successfully bolstering the peso against market pressures. The presumption of an overvaluation of the currency was based on terms of purchasing power parity, supplemented by anecdotal evidence of high wage growth and declining export profits. Those points were always indisputable, especially in the presence of large external deficits combined with low economic growth, as Table 2.1 shows. Nevertheless, what mattered in the short run is that the markets viewed the Salinas government as fully committed to defending the peso.

The defense consisted of tightening monetary policy, which would dry up liquidity as interest rates rose, making any speculation against the peso extremely costly. On top of this short-term policy, government policymakers argued that the medium-term macroeconomic policy would bring further structural reforms and sound public finances, and they convinced the markets that stability would be the ultimate outcome. Accordingly, the focus of policy was to ensure a falling inflation rate, which would raise the prospects of high yields for foreign investors as long as interest rates remained high and the peso stable within a preestablished fluctuation band. The external deficit was deemed a temporary phenomenon; the peso overvaluation could be disputed in the light of high export growth; and in the end, further structural reforms would make the peso even more competitive.

Those arguments were credible to many, especially given the Salinas cabinet's considerable reputation for having stabilized the economy during the Salinas term. Thus, foreign investors saw their confidence renewed after short periods of uncertainty. Nevertheless, in the short run, as the administration tightened monetary policy, nominal yields on government securities would rise, and the peso would appreciate in real terms. Investors who bet against the peso lost on both counts, which gradually made peso instruments irresistible and maximized the inflows of portfolio capital in 1993. Since in the short run market confidence is always more important than economic fundamentals in determining the fate of currencies, the government was less concerned with examining the arguments of those who pointed to the economic fundamentals.

The administration's approach proved successful in dealing with currency uncertainty in 1993, while the U.S. Congress was debating whether to approve NAFTA. And so it was in 1994 as well, despite a series of destabilizing events: the Zapatista uprising, which began in January and remained unresolved at year's end; the assassination of ruling party (PRI) candidate Luis Donaldo Colosio, in March; the sudden resignation of the respected secretary of the interior, Jorge Carpizo, in June; and Deputy Attorney General Mario Ruiz Massieu's serious allegations of PRI complicity in the assassination of his brother, José Francisco Ruiz Massieu, in September. Although players in the financial markets knew that the peso was overvalued, they also knew that the key in the short run was that the Salinas administration was fully prepared to provoke liquidity shortages in order to bolster the peso. What they did not know was that this policy would be challenged during the transition to the new administration, especially as the president-elect had given every signal that he would not keep Pedro Aspe at the finance ministry. Foreign investors also ignored the vocal complaints of various political groups regarding the lack of economic growth, which were indirectly weakening the policy stance of the government during the presidential campaign. In fact, as 1994 progressed, the government had started to relax its tight fiscal policy, while the Bank of Mexico loosened monetary controls and became more accommodating to the economic expansion, which explains the reduction in net portfolio inflows although a massive withdrawal of foreign funds did not occur.

Notwithstanding obscure information from the government—even to date—on the true extent of the fiscal relaxation, foreign investors were growing suspicious of the administration. They therefore did not increase their holdings of Mexican paper in 1994 as they had during the previous year. On the contrary, in responding to their doubts, the government had issued a large number of *tesobonos* (dollar-denominated short-term bonds) to ease the way for investors to drop their peso risk without altogether losing their position in Mexico. Investors responded by switching almost completely out of *cetes* (peso-denominated short-term bonds) and into *tesobonos.* For that reason, the value of *tesobonos* jumped from U.S.$1.4 billion in January 1994 to $30.4 billion in December, while that of *cetes* fell from $22.7 billion to $5.4 billion. Thus, of the $14 billion increase in *tesobono* holdings by foreigners during the year, $10 billion represented a switch away from *cetes*. The shift was ongoing, most notably after Colosio's assassination at the end of March. Even so, a year later, President Zedillo would assert, "I was not aware, for one thing, of how fast the structure of the domestic debt had changed. . . . I became aware of the *tesobono* problem in December."[3] If that is true, according to Aspe's published story, then he had asked President Salinas to devalue the peso in November while not knowing what the level of dollar-indexed government debt was.

Market credibility during Salinas's years was also enhanced by the unconditional support granted to the government by private sector leaders in Mexico. Since those leaders have traditionally been very close to the government, and all of them had recently benefited from the policy of privatization and expanded access to foreign capital markets, their faith in the government was total. For one thing, the private sector in Mexico has rarely had a prescient sense of the implications of macroeconomic policy, as was demonstrated in the oil boom and crisis of the 1970s. For another, it has never encouraged independent economic analysis within its own think tanks or even in the economic departments of the large corporations. Hence, it is not surprising that as the fiscal relaxation was reflected in high economic growth and large increases in central bank lending, in the face of plummeting external financing, the president of the Mexican Bankers Association, Roberto Hernández, predicted that interest rates would also plunge as soon as Zedillo became president. That was but one of numerous examples of the strong belief among business leaders that holding the peso within the preset band depended on the government's will—a belief that seemed to ignore important warnings emanating from the United States about insufficient foreign funds for Mexico.

Although it is true that much of the impetus for foreign capital inflows would depend on the depth and pace of Mexico's domestic economic reforms, it was open to discussion whether the reforms had thus far been deep enough. Mexican business leaders generally believed, wrongly, that the government was doing all that was necessary. Therefore, they tended to respond to claims of currency overvaluation by repeating the same line as that tendered by the government: that recent growth in manufacturing exports proved that the structural reforms were on the right track and thus the current policy was sufficient. The International Monetary Fund (IMF) made the same mistake as recently as in its October 1994 internal review of Mexico. To make the arguments against peso risks even stronger, some investors argued that the Bank of Mexico was now autonomous. Such an interpretation was exceedingly sanguine, for the changes in the bank's legislation passed by the congress in 1993 were in fact only minor. Indeed, in the broader context of Mexican institutions generally, the changes did not amount to any different political arrangement over and above what had existed until then. For example, in the new legislation, the government retained the power to decide the exchange rate policy even though the bank was given a vague mandate to "protect the purchasing power" of the peso.[4]

This tenuous state of affairs was made even more tenuous by the fact that the new economic team of President Zedillo was in many ways seen as completely new and thus uninvolved with these issues, despite having been a part of the Salinas cabinet. Apart from the fissures already mentioned, the fact that Zedillo's cabinet failed to inspire confidence in the continuity of economic reform became the real problem for the peso in December, the first month of the new presidency. To a large degree, that crisis of confidence could have been avoided if the Zedillo team had appreciated the fact that during the second half of 1994 the current-account deficit averaging U.S.$2.5 billion per month was partly financed out of international reserves. Ignoring the implications of that shortfall, the new administration concentrated its efforts on obtaining congressional approval for the 1995 budget, instead of developing a strategic plan to deal with the peso problem.

Again, Pedro Aspe's detailed revelations about the November 20 meeting confirm this interpretation. In response to the Zedillo request to devalue the peso, Aspe predictably defended his policy with exactly the same arguments he had used during the previous three years. Since those arguments had had plenty of time to be proven wrong or at least suspect, it is amazing that they were enough to stop the new government from insisting on a devaluation and, indeed, from implementing one as soon as Zedillo was inaugurated in early December. This suggests that the Zedillo team was short of conviction on *any* macroeconomic policy.

Thus, the market mounted a massive speculative attack against the peso on the announcement of the lifting of the band, as it concluded that the government would lack sufficient understanding of market conditions and internal coordination to maintain it as promised. Only one day after Serra Puche hailed the new band as offering more flexibility, the authorities had to let the peso float, in light of the heavy reserve losses that made the peso plunge another 40 percent. The management of the institutional aspects of that change in regime was probably worse than the event itself. Although all the details have not been revealed to the public, the fact that Serra Puche consulted the members of the Anti-Inflation Pact (business and labor) on the exchange rate policy to follow displayed great weakness in the new government. The business sector is known to have insisted on the government's sustaining the peso within the new and wider 15 percent band, which it did. In practice, this meant that the government offered a cheap-dollar window that speculators used to cause further losses in reserves. And in the end, those decisions brought about the breakdown of the Anti-Inflation Pact itself, which had been in successful existence since 1987.

All told, the medium-term strategy of the Salinas administration was inappropriately risky and bound to fail sooner or later, but in its short-run management of the devaluation, the Zedillo administration bears greater responsibility for the debacle.

The verdict must therefore be that although the outgoing administration left a serious problem behind, the Zedillo team's management of the transition was exceedingly ill informed and shortsighted. Granted, the Salinas government must still be credited for the structural reforms it undertook, which had created a good business climate. But that result must not be confused with a steady-state situation without any need for further adjustment. The error of most market analysts was that they thought an exchange rate adjustment was incompatible with the desired economic reforms, ignoring the fact that reform is a structural process of several stages. Thus, when the exchange rate is pegged to a strong currency as a tool of macroeconomic stabilization, structural reforms must then proceed at high speed. Only structural reforms can offset increases in domestic over international costs. Since a pegged exchange rate, fixed or quasi-fixed, provides little room for adjustment, domestic cost increases make the economy lose competitiveness until such reforms reduce costs, deregulate the economy, and create more competition. In other words, the reforms are necessary not only to modernize the economy, but also to validate the pegged exchange rate over the medium term.

Flaws in the Salinas Economic Model

Before examining what would have averted the debacle that followed the devaluation, let us first review four main flaws in the theoretical underpinnings of the Salinas strategy.

One was the notion that a large current-account deficit is nothing but the result of foreign capital inflows. According to this narrow view, foreign investment was attracted to Mexico by favorable business expectations. Since the private sector "knows what it is doing," the argument goes, when capital inflows stop, domestic investment falls, imports are reduced, and the deficit is automatically corrected. The government therefore should not be concerned by a large deficit.

This view became dominant in Mexico despite its having been discredited four years earlier in the United Kingdom, where Chancellor of the Exchequer Nigel Lawson had articulated it in the late 1980s. Blind faith in the automatic adjustment led the private sector to continue spending and generating ever higher deficits. Mexican banks used their foreign borrowing to finance domestic consumption and the investments of their Mexican clients.

This dubious argument was built around the axiom that after the fact and over the long run, the balance of the capital account on the balance of payments is always equal to the balance on the current account. But an accounting equation was misused as a guideline calling for a policy of neglect. Indeed, the equation has nothing to say about what the domestic economy does with the capital inflow. The deficit that follows the initial capital inflow will in fact depend on the investment and consumption decisions of the private sector—if we assume that the public sector maintains an unchanged fiscal balance. In other words, the deficit over the next period contains the result of *changed* domestic activity, i.e., the posited equation ceases to reflect only the effect of a foreign capital inflow.

For the purposes of economic policymaking it is this change that is relevant, for it may reveal an unsustainable level of activity in the private sector that the government may want to alter through fiscal or monetary policy. It may also unmask faulty assumptions by economic agents, stemming from a distorted price system. For example, the exchange rate may be overvalued, causing market actors to engage in increased consumption of imports and increased foreign borrowing, when both activities in reality imply the assumption of great risks by the private sector.

The argument concocted by the authorities also overlooked the fact that the transition from a high external deficit to a low one after capital inflows stop is usually not a smooth one. For example, when the private sector invests in projects that are not completed by the time the capital inflows stop, the investors will try to borrow at higher rates of interest in order to complete the projects. And when the projects are completed, the market value of the investment may suffer if the project relied on a high level of consumption; in other words, this value is likely to be reduced as a result of the reduced capital inflow. The obvious result is a loss in private wealth. If the adjustment involves a currency devaluation, the loss is magnified. And if, in addition, the banking system is overgeared, the resulting lack of liquidity will make the adjustment much more difficult than is implied by the proponents of the "automatic adjustment" argument.

A second flaw in the Salinas administration's strategy was its argument that Mexican productivity growth would offset the appreciation of the peso in real terms. This was the same as saying that the increase in domestic costs in excess of international costs (both measured in dollars) was canceled by the higher growth in productivity. The administration would cite the high growth in exports, but it failed to see that wages, in dollar terms, were increasing at a very high rate, not only in export industries but in every sector. Thus, if exporters recorded steady exports but at the same time were covering these increases in domestic costs, they would reap lower profits. In fact, this situation was common among exporters, but they kept exporting because they had long-term contracts or because their domestic sales were depressed. Meanwhile, the government seemed to have lost track of export profitability.

But even the record on Mexican productivity growth was not that impressive if placed in the proper context. Table 2.3 shows that although productivity rose faster in Mexico than in the United States and other developed nations (as one would expect of an emerging economy), it nonetheless fell short of growth rates in other emerging markets, such as China and Korea. Compared to the appreciation of the exchange rates of these countries vis-à-vis the dollar, the peso recorded a higher real appreciation, which was apparently not offset by the nation's higher productivity. But even if a high differential between rates of productivity growth in Mexico and the United States justified maintaining Mexico's exchange rate policy, a broader examination of productivity trends would have strongly suggested the need for additional structural reforms. The high growth in wages measured in dollars, highlighted in Table 2.2, combined with the appreciation of the peso, suggests that Mexican labor may not have been competitive.

Table 2.4 further develops this point. The Salinas administration and, in its 1994 annual report, the Bank of Mexico, had argued that growth in Mexican exports surpassed that of efficient Asian countries over the years 1990–1994. To the bank's information (first column), I have added the column on gross domestic product (GDP) growth during the same period, which reveals that in Mexico such high growth failed to trickle down to the rest of the economy. Specifically, despite its 74.6 percent increase in exports, Mexico recorded only a 16.0 percent growth in GDP. Singapore,

Table 2.3   Accumulated Percentage Increase in Productivity from 1990 to 1994 in Mexico and Other Selected Countries

Country	
Mexico	22.6
United States	4.1
Germany	13.5
Japan	–4.0
Spain	11.3
Chile	18.0
Argentina	26.6
Korea	40.7
Singapore	32.2
China	43.9

Sources: Bank of Mexico, Annual Report 1994 (Mexico City: Bank of Mexico, 1995); International Monetary Fund, International Financial Statistics (Washington, D.C.: International Monetary Fund Publications, July 1995).

Table 2.4   Percentage Increase in Exports and GDP of Mexico and Other Selected Countries Between 1990 and 1994

Country	% Increase in Exports in Current U.S. $	% Increase in Constant Prices for GDP
Mexico	74.6	16.0
United States	27.7	10.5
Germany	–5.6	13.7
Japan	38.0	11.5
Spain	31.7	7.7
Chile	37.8	36.2
Argentina	27.3	34.4
Korea	48.1	43.9
Taiwan	33.4	36.5
Singapore	83.5	46.0
Hong Kong	84.8	26.4
China	97.5	61.7

Sources: Bank of Mexico, *Annual Report 1994* (Mexico City: Bank of Mexico, 1995); International Monetary Fund, *International Financial Statistics* (Washington, D.C.: International Monetary Fund Publications, July 1995).

Hong Kong, and China had similarly high growth in exports but, by contrast, much higher growth in GDP. And Argentina and Chile, which recorded milder growth in exports, had more than twice as much growth in GDP as Mexico. Either the rest of Mexico's economy was not doing as well as its exporters, or the export sector was too small to pull up the rest of the economy. But whichever the cause, the government's use of export indicators to make a case for the absence of an exchange rate problem lacks analytical value.

A third misguided argument, also repeated in the 1994 Bank of Mexico report, was that a developing country may carry large external deficits for a long period of time before suffering negative consequences. The government again resorted to the examples of Singapore, Malaysia, and Thailand. Those countries, however, were not exhibiting the high growth in consumption nor in bank lending for consumption that Mexico exhibited in its brief period of high deficits. Instead, all three invested heavily in manufacturing capacity, which later on became exports, supported by much higher rates of savings than Mexico has ever achieved. By contrast, the evidence in other countries much more similar to Mexico, such as Spain, Australia, Canada, Italy, and Turkey, is that those countries have been unable to maintain high deficits for more than a few years.

The fourth flaw in the Salinas economic model was its argument that the privatization of state entities should be done with the aim of maximizing revenues to the state. Since in many cases the entities to be privatized either were not previously regulated or their sector of activity was deregulated, monopolistic rents were tolerated—for example, in the privatized telephone and banking sectors.

Mexican banks deserve specific mention. Because the privatized banks were sold at overvalued prices—and those costs could not be recouped in an environment of increasing competition and sluggish economic growth—the new owners had to resort to nonbank operations to generate the larger part of their profits. Those transactions involved taking risks that otherwise, under sound financial practices, would have been avoided. In 1992, for example, the banks were excessively exposed to inflation-indexed bonds *(ajustabonos),* which dropped in value as interest rates jumped in the summer, causing enormous losses that took several years to absorb. And in 1993/94, given their belief that the peso exchange rate would be maintained, many bankers had uncovered exposure in U.S. dollars. Now that the government must rescue many of these same institutions from bankruptcy, the "revenue" it received from their sale is likely to be exceeded by the costs of the rescue, refuting the prime goal of the privatization strategy.

How Preventable Was the
Economic Debacle Following the Devaluation?

With the benefit of hindsight, eighteen months after the devaluation, I can say that smooth transition planning in the Zedillo team was not the order of the day. The critical needs for rapidly getting up to speed on market developments as they were known to the Salinas team and for establishing clear and open lines of communication with the U.S. government and market participants simply were not met during the first months of the Zedillo administration.

Since the economy was vulnerable, in the light of economic fundamentals, it should not have been difficult for the Zedillo team to conclude that further structural reform was necessary. This was true whether Zedillo's planners wished to defend the exchange rate in the terms specified in the Salinas strategy and the Anti-Inflation Pact or, instead, if they wished to modify the policy. Continuing with economic reforms necessarily involved a critical view of the Salinas reforms, which had protected vested interests and which had been delayed in order to negotiate some reciprocity from the U.S. government through NAFTA. In 1995, however, it was absolutely essential to institute policies promoting access to foreign direct investment in telecommunications, banking, and financial services and reforming labor markets, social security, and pensions. In fact, the need for these policies was all the greater as the peso exchange rate became vulnerable to speculative attacks.

Announcing those kinds of reforms would have provided fundamental support for the peso and indeed for any change in policy. President Zedillo had a prime opportunity to do so on December 1, 1994, in his inaugural speech. Unfortunately, although he touched on the subject, he failed to signal any emphatic commitment.

Having wasted that opportunity, the president had a second chance when he announced on December 29 the first policies to accompany the devaluation. That occasion was also propitious because at that time many market players were still under the impression that Mexican equities were now cheaper. Nonetheless, the president failed here too, and the announcement of reforms came only piecemeal later on, when the financial community was much more worried about the prospect of Mexico's default on its foreign debt.

Also missing in the administration's public profile was a presidential cabinet strongly identified with and committed to further market reform. Unlike the young members of the Salinas team who had just such an identification and commitment, Zedillo's cabinet included many old-guard members of the ruling Institutional Revolutionary Party (PRI), who were not at all identified with the thrust of the Salinas reforms.

To understand the need for an early reshuffling of the cabinet, we must note that Salinas was successful in restructuring the economy and attracting foreign capital largely because he made the economic agenda the precise central motive around which his cabinet was organized. Nothing in Salinas's political or social programs nor in his international dealings made full sense independent of the economic agenda. If President Zedillo had maintained the same preeminence of economic issues, he would have had a much better chance of maintaining the impetus of reform and especially the peso exchange rate. Although the exchange rate was not cast in iron, any alteration of it had to be managed very carefully and sold as part of ongoing structural reforms.

Contrary to what the public debate in Mexico suggests today—that President Zedillo had very little room for maneuvering—I believe a variety of options were open to him. For example, while reaffirming the continuity of the reform objectives, he could also have defined a more advanced version of the economic agenda that would have won the confidence of investors. Given that kind of agenda, an exchange rate devaluation would in fact have fit well. Indeed, it was the opinion of many foreign direct investors that a devaluation was desirable to restore a level of relative prices conducive to domestic production and greater exports.

The 1995 Macroeconomic Strategy:
Perched on a Slippery Slope

It is not difficult to consider the current economic program of adjustment as an emergency, short-term plan, when one recalls that it was the third program elaborated by the Zedillo administration in as many months. In

December 1994, the finance secretary, Serra Puche, presented the first program to the congress, which elaborated a 5 percent target for inflation, a 4 percent target for GDP growth, and no change in the exchange rate policy, that is, no nominal devaluation above that set in the established band. The second program, elaborated in early January 1995, had an inflation target of 19.5 percent, a growth target of 1.5 percent, no explicit target for the exchange rate, and a reduction of the external current-account deficit from U.S.$29 billion to $14 billion; the IMF endorsed this program.

The third program was issued in February as a result of the loan agreement signed with the U.S. government that same month. Received with great skepticism, partly because the two previous programs had failed to instill confidence in the markets and partly because of the bad management of the devaluation, the third program had to overstate the degree of economic adjustment in 1995 in order to be convincing. In particular, it proposed an exceedingly large drop in domestic consumer demand and the external deficit.

As shown in Table 2.5, the government targets of the program included an inflation rate in December 1995 of 42 percent (which represents an average inflation of about 34 percent). Minimum wages would be allowed to increase by 19.8 percent, with a second rise to be granted in April. Taking into account the different timings of the wage increases and the continuous rise in prices, I estimate real wages to have fallen by 16 percent during the year. Household income should fall by 14 percent, assuming that the main income is always supplemented by a smaller second income but also that job losses will affect at least 10 percent of the labor force. All told, the ambitious target for reducing the current-account deficit—from U.S.$28.5 billion to $2.3 billion, or about 10 percent of GDP—was feasible and in fact was exceeded, as preliminary estimates for the deficit are approximately $1 billion.

The government's projection of a drop in GDP of 2 percent in 1995 must therefore be understood as a combined result of the real wage and external adjustments. Nonetheless, to begin implementing the policies conducive to these targets, Mexico first needed the $20 billion in U.S. loans and $17.8 billion in IMF loans pledged in February 1995 to facilitate an orderly redemption of the *tesobonos* held by foreigners (which amounted to $18 billion) and other short-term obligations that were unlikely to be renewed. The latter included commercial banks' certificates of deposit, interbank obligations, private sector short-term maturities in Eurobonds, and a small part of public sector debt.

Since the program anticipates a degree of domestic sacrifice that is likely to involve substantial loss of wealth and serious barriers to a subsequent recovery, it cannot be enforced for more than the short term. The very degree of expected adjustment seems inconsistent with what both the United States and the IMF predicated in their loan agreements—that the

Table 2.5   The Mexican Government's Economic Targets for Calendar Years 1993–1995 and the Author's Estimates for 1995

Economic Target	1993	1994	1995 Program Estimate[a]	Estimated Outcome
Growth and prices				
GDP real change (%)	0.6	3.5	−2.0	−8
Nominal GDP (NPs, billions)	1,123	1,245	1,669	1,466
GDP (U.S., billions)	356	374	278	232
Inflation (Dec.–Dec., %)	8.0	7.1	42.0	52.0
Consumption (real % change)	0.4	2.3	n.a.	−15.0
Investment (real % change)	−1.2	9.9	n.a.	−30.0
Public finances (% of GDP)				
Financial balance	0.7	−0.3	0.5	−1.5
Primary budget surplus	3.9	2.3	4.4	2.5
Budget revenue	25.7	25.5	25.6	24.0
Spending on programs	18.4	19.7	18.2	18.0
Debt interest	3.1	2.6	3.9	5.0
Financial Variables (annual % change)				
Exchange rate average (NPs/U.S.$)	3.1554	3.3325	6.000	6.5
Minimum wages, Dec. (NPs per day)	14.3	15.3	19.8	19.8
Balance of payments (U.S.$, millions)				
Current account	−23,399	−28,786	−2,376	−1,000
Imports of goods	65,367	79,346	69,944	72,900
Non-oil exports	44,468	52,876	n.a.	71,500
Volume of oil exports (millions of barrels per day)	1.354	1.338	n.a.	1.3
Oil price (dollars per barrel)[b]	13.2	13.6	n.a.	15.0

Sources: Presidency of the Republic, *Criterios de Política Económica* (Mexico City: Presidency of the Republic, various years); Bank of Mexico.

[a]Program for 1995 denotes the targets in the government program issued in February 1995 once it acknowledged that the devaluation would oblige it to a radical adjustment and insufficient foreign finance to a more radical one.

[b]Basket of Mexican crudes.

state of the economy is inherently good and that the crisis was merely caused by a temporary shortage of financing. But if that was their belief, it stands against reason that they demanded a program in which the domestic economy must eliminate a deficit of 8 percent of GDP on its external accounts in a single year while continuing to meet its short-term foreign obligations.

There are in fact two main problems with the current economic program. One is a moral issue that can be enunciated quite simply as an unfair distribution of the burden of the adjustment between the domestic economy and the foreign investors, as well as among socioeconomic groups within Mexico. In redeeming foreign holdings of *tesobonos* with the funds borrowed from the United States and the IMF and ensuring their convertibility into dollars, the Mexican government was in effect immunizing foreign investors against the substantial market risks they themselves took. And in so validating the misguided investments of foreign entities, the government went even further, automatically converting a peso debt into a dollar debt; a debt owed to private funds into a debt owed to the U.S. government; and a debt with no guarantee into a debt backed by Mexico's oil reserves. All of those acts of conversion took place with no loss to the foreign holders—hardly a precedent to make them more cautious in the future.

Worse, to make the loan repayment feasible, the Mexican people will suffer a deep and widespread loss in welfare, not only in wage cuts and job losses, but also in stagnant employment growth, rising interest rates on their debt, and increased crime and social tensions. This is the second fundamental problem with the economic program. The losses in real wages and employment should provoke a fall in economic activity in the range of 8 percent in 1995—the result of tax increases, inflation in excess of wage increases (known as the inflation tax), and higher interest rates, all compounded by the reduction in public and private spending. A socioeconomic adjustment of that magnitude is even greater than those adjustments experienced during the foreign debt crises in 1983 and 1986. Moreover, the current one has new features because it also involves low inflation and a reduction in the real stock of money. The monetary base contracted by 43 percent in real terms from December through October.

In other words, with lack of liquidity, which is partly attributable to the strict conditions of the U.S. loan package, the prices of sellers must plunge to facilitate a clearing in the market. Since producers (like workers who must work for some pay) need to repay their debt, their products and assets must be liquidated at prices way below their actual value. Many producers will undergo heavy losses because many of their projects are incomplete. And banks will lose large sums on their outstanding loans. All told, these eventualities add up to a prolonged recession for the Mexican economy.

Meanwhile, the government wants to raise the level of domestic savings, the lack of which can largely explain the 1994 crisis; but it is brushing aside the fact that the savings rate took nearly six years to drop to its present low level and simply will not rise quickly. Furthermore, increasing savings by forcing consumption down with the inflation tax has already proven to be an unsustainable strategy; it worked briefly in the 1980s only to have the problem recur in the 1990s. The government is not taking into account the fundamental axiom of Keynesian economics—that any sustainable increase in the volume of savings originates from a higher national income. Thus, given the other implications of the administration's program for employment, output, and private wealth, and the absence of any program for the medium term, it is difficult to see any promise in the president's strategy to boost the savings rate.

Mexican banks are, of course, a casualty of their own extremely im-
prudent management as well as of the deep postdevaluation slump in the
economy. The 1995 program accentuated the problems of financial institutions, as it offered no cushion against excessive deflationary forces.

To avoid prolonging the recession, the authorities should instead focus
on achieving a direct reduction in interest rates; the current focus on a
nominal exchange rate is more in the interest of foreign creditors. But if
Mexico has established collateral, such as its oil revenues, this provides a
reasonable assurance of repayment to the U.S. government. Therefore, the
management of domestic financial policies should be guided by domestic
considerations instead of external ones. Formulating policy priorities the
other way around may soon cause an early and premature appreciation of
the peso, without relieving the Mexican people of the burden of the adjustment. That effect is readily predictable because of the way in which a
tight monetary policy operates. As it raises interest rates, it also exacer-
bates the economic slump, reducing income and the demand for money
and strengthening the exchange rate. The result is a higher than expected
return on short-term financial savings, which serves to attract more funds
of this sort but not, ironically, long-term investment, since what investors
see is continued recession and structural weakness.

In addition, although nominal interest rates may fall in this kind of environment, the real ex ante interest rate has fallen much less, further dis-
couraging investment and future output and employment. True, the combination of some renewed capital inflows and a peso that has appreciated in
real terms is a good signal for short-term capital, but it has an ominous effect on the domestic economy.

I have attempted a preliminary estimation of the loss of private wealth
involved in the present Mexican deflation. The analysis is based on a consideration of actual price and value movements in private assets and ig-
nores many small forms of losses in wealth by concentrating on the main
sectors of the economy: the portfolios of commercial banks, the equity investments of the public, and the foreign exchange positions of Mexican
borrowers. My estimation is intended as a broad indication of potential
magnitudes and not as a precise quantification of losses. For that reason, I
concentrate on one part of the paper loss, that which is likely to materialize during 1995–1996.

Specifically, I estimate that the total loss of wealth to the Mexican
people and Mexican institutions will be, conservatively speaking, U.S.$45
billion, or 16 percent of GDP. That total—estimated for the period running
from December 19, 1994, to the end of 1996—is based on the following
assumptions and calculations.

1. The private sector, excluding banks, had $30 billion in foreign debt.
Since most bank credit was directed to peso-revenue projects (assumed to

be two-thirds of bank credit), which will be impossible to recoup over the next two years, a likely loss of 50 percent would translate into $15 billion.

2. I have elsewhere estimated the overdue portfolio of Mexican banks at $30 billion; several bankers with whom I have discussed the estimate concur with the figure. If we assume no further deterioration in the portfolios, a likely loss of 50 percent to private shareholders would represent $15 billion. The scale of support some of those banks have received from the Mexican government (so far, $5 billion in direct support and an unknown amount in indirect support) suggests that the total loss may be in fact greater.

3. The loss in equities from November 30, 1994, to December 1995 was $73 billion, excluding the holdings of foreign investors. If we assume that one-fifth of that loss will materialize within the first year after the devaluation, as investors need to liquidate debts or creditors to execute guarantees, the loss would be $15 billion.

Even a total loss of $45 billion seems small if Mexico's high interest rates continue for very long. Of course, part of the loss is now taking the form of continued injections of domestic credit granted to commercial and development banks by the Bank of Mexico. That credit is not monetized, however, as the banks are using it to increase their reserves, which they then deposit in the Bank of Mexico. Nonetheless, the potential effect on the fiscal deficit is very high, in case the Bank of Mexico has to take over such banks. Until now, all of the banks privatized in 1991–1992 have received credit from the Bank of Mexico.

It is the extent of the destruction of private wealth that will make it necessary for the government to relax its monetary policy in 1996. Nonetheless, a simple relaxation, without a strategy for the future, will present serious risks, for there will be many sectors of the economy demanding financial support. Moreover, in responding to those demands, the government may be tempted to mix fiscal with monetary relaxation, causing an early appreciation of the peso that can only be followed by a future weakening of the currency. And throughout, the government will never convince the markets that it has a consistent strategy for the medium term.

Mexican Views of the U.S. Loan Package and Its Long-Term Implications

Since the bulk of the financing obtained from the U.S. government and the IMF has been earmarked to repay short-term foreign debt, especially the *tesobono* obligations, the prevalent view in Mexico is that the United States was more interested in bailing out portfolio investors than in supporting the Mexican economy. Of course, that distinction is highly politicized and not necessarily true, but the fact is that both governments will have to deal with the political consequences of the perception.

In its actual specifics, the U.S. loan package consists of short-term swaps through which Mexico borrows dollars for ninety days; medium-term swaps, for up to five years; and guarantees for Mexican government securities for up to ten years. Mexico will pay interest for the medium-term swaps at U.S. ninety-one-day treasury bill rates, plus 225 to 375 basis points "or more," depending on the term. For the guarantees, Mexico will pay the difference between the risk-free interest rate and the original rate, plus 225 to 375 basis points "or more," although the exact point in the range is not clear in the agreement.

Apart from the package's strict conditions to use the loans "to retire, refinance, or restructure short-term obligations," the agreement contains economic targets as conditions for the maintenance of the support: negative real growth of money, a fiscal surplus of 0.5 percent of GDP, and further privatizations and structural reforms.

Many of the provisions of the U.S. loan agreement are in the interest of Mexico to pursue, but only in the short term, as was mentioned above, and not without taking into consideration the more important domestic economic conditions. The present involvement of U.S. financial authorities in monitoring and determining the stance of Mexico's macroeconomic policy is fraught with political risk, especially given the precedent the agreement itself set of bailing out private investors. By the same token, investors now expect the U.S. authorities to give Mexico the seal of approval on its policies. But those policies face serious challenges over the next two years if the slump continues and becomes a deep recession. It is therefore in the interest of the U.S. authorities to disengage from the short-run management of Mexico's economy and to insist that the IMF prescribe appropriate policies for interest rates and for an early resumption of economic growth. At this moment, however, that may be a tall order, for the fact is that consensus on economic prescriptions between IMF analysts and Washington policymakers has been broken by the Mexican crisis. In other words, there may not be a new economic model to be prescribed.

There is no question that Mexico did try to follow the right restructuring model for a bloated public sector and a closed economy during the late 1980s and early 1990s. Nevertheless, the government did not restructure certain key parts of the economy, such as assets and labor, which left distortions in markets that rendered the model risky and socially unfair. Yet the IMF and the World Bank never expressed reservations about that lack of fulfillment. Even today there is little admission that the strategy was flawed, and much of the economic debate in Mexico is still permeated by dogma. And so we find, in some circles where there is a fear of admitting the faults of the strategy, the discussion is still about whether Mexico should have devalued or not.

Across the border in the United States, we can also still find discussion of the wrongheaded notion that a hard currency can be maintained by the will of the monetary authority. Apart from representing an extremely limited and superseded school of economic thought, this type of proposition confuses the markets, for it makes them believe that varying the nominal exchange rate was *a choice* of the Mexican government. Thus, we find parties on both sides of the border distracted from the medium-term structural issues—which should be the highest priority in efforts to develop an enhanced model of economic reform.

Conclusions

The most critical ingredient missing from the Mexican economic program (and often from other programs where there is a systematic exchange rate appreciation during stabilization) is the synchronized liberalization of *all markets:* goods, capital, assets, and labor. Mexico failed to liberalize the asset market by setting constraints on foreign equity investment and by protecting domestic monopolies. It also failed to liberalize the labor market.

With the Mexican model in question, the IMF and World Bank lacking a concrete blueprint for further economic reform, and consensus building in Washington at a standstill, there is now an intellectual vacuum. Any stabilization policies pursued are therefore likely to follow an ad hoc, short-term rule. Not only are Mexico's economic prospects threatened as a result, but NAFTA itself is beginning to lose its luster as a promising long-term development project for the hemisphere.

In a world of flexible policies and ad hoc, short-term rules, there is little room for the Bretton Woods institutions, except for some lending by the World Bank. It is therefore not difficult to anticipate a declining influence of these institutions in the developing world, especially since their standing in Europe has already been seriously damaged. As a result, a concomitant loss of influence for the United States can also be anticipated.

For Mexico itself, the long-term consequences of the peso crisis are likely to range wide and deep within the society. First, given the extensive losses of private wealth, it must be a new generation of entrepreneurs and bankers that takes the leading role in the next economic recovery. That leadership will take time to emerge, unless Mexico opens up in a dramatic fashion to foreign direct investment and at the same time deregulates the economy to provide a level playing field for Mexican entrepreneurs. Whether encouraged by the government or not, such new entrepreneurs would define the shape of a possible new alliance between the state and private capital in Mexico. If a new generation of capitalists managed to emerge in the wake of the debt crisis of the 1980s and that represented a significant change at that time, any such change now should prove even more dramatic. The new entrepreneurs are likely to be smaller and more closely involved in manufacturing, farming, and niche sectors. Politically, they are likely to be farther removed from the government and the ruling PRI than their predecessors, as well as more impatient with piecemeal economic and political reform. But these entrepreneurs are also likely to find workers and the middle class generally in a more disaffected mood than the labor and consumer markets that held sway in the late 1980s and early 1990s. There is no question that over the past fifteen years entrepreneurs have become more vocal in their criticism against the government as a result of the various economic crises. This was the case even in the best years of the Salinas administration when NAFTA promised to deliver great gains for the economy. The reason is that the adjustment from a closed to an open economy often hurt business, especially the small and medium-sized businesses.

With the advent of another period of adjustment on top of heavy losses, entrepreneurs will become much more cautious and skeptical of any governmental grand plan. Their confidence in the government and the PRI being shattered will fragment them as a political group. This is likely to result in greater political participation at the regional level and in less willingness to support the central government. That is why the National Action Party (PAN), which usually caters to this segment of society, has been so successful in local elections in places where there is a large representation of small business.

The likely course of events, given the government's need for fresh resources, is that foreign investors and banks will be allowed to take key positions in the economy. This would dramatically alter the balance of political forces in Mexico. Although it would likely alleviate the problems of insufficient economic activity and employment and eventually gain the support of the middle class and the small entrepreneur, any heightened foreign profile would also encounter stiff opposition from big business in Mexico. There is little the government can do to avoid a significant increase of foreign ownership in Mexico, and it would be wrong to delay solutions to the economic slump because of considerations for big business. Still, vested interest mainly in private business (bankers, monopolies, large traditional industrial groups) will try to press the government to avoid a full opening of the economy; and they may succeed in the short term, especially if the government is weak and requires the backing of business, among other groups, to ensure political stability. Nevertheless, in the medium term, the opening is inevitable and no coalition of forces would be capable of preventing it and at the same time ensure economic growth.

Notes

1. Tim Golden, "Mexico's New Leader Finds Job Full of Painful Surprises," *New York Times,* March 14, 1995, p. A1.

2. Pedro Aspe, "México en 1994: Las razones de la política cambiaria," *Reforma,* July 15, 1995.

3. Golden, "Mexico's New Leader."

4. Juan Carlos Torres, "The Mexican Money Market," *Latin Finance,* no. 54 (January 1994): S20.

3

The Mexican Devaluation and the U.S. Response: Potomac Politics, 1995-Style

Riordan Roett

The mismanaged devaluation of the Mexican peso on December 20, 1994, sent a massive shock wave through global financial circles. Although the markets appeared more sanguine about the situation by mid-1996, a number of questions remain regarding what led to the devaluation, what participants in the Mexican market should have known, and how the actual decision to devalue was made and implemented. Damage control after the fact proceeded on two fronts. One was in Mexico City, with the new government of President Ernesto Zedillo Ponce de León. The second was in Washington, D.C., where the Clinton administration sought to grapple with the implications of the devaluation—for both the United States and the international financial system as a whole. After examining the prelude and early responses to the crisis, this chapter analyzes the Clinton administration's initial efforts to build a bipartisan coalition in Congress to support loan guarantees for Mexico, the failure of that emergency plan, the second emergency response, and the political fallout from the policy process pursued by the Democratic administration in seeking Republican support in Congress.

The Origins of the Crisis

Assessments of the new Mexican administration were generally positive throughout Washington in December 1994. Zedillo's appointment of individuals like Jaime Serra Puche and Guillermo Ortiz to key decisionmaking positions was reassuring. Both were well known and respected in the U.S. capital, Serra Puche as the chief Mexican negotiator of the North American Trade Agreement (NAFTA) of 1993, and Ortiz as secretary for communications and transport. Zedillo's inaugural address on December 1 had been stronger and more appealing than expected, particularly his calls for greater political democracy, legal reform, and a final clarification of the series of political assassinations that had plagued the country over the previous eighteen months. Serra Puche, as the new finance minister, signaled that there would be little change in Mexico's economic policy under Zedillo, and he vigorously denied any inclination to devalue the peso.[1]

Also welcome to Washington observers was Zedillo's announcement, in a nationally televised speech in mid-December, of a multiparty legislative commission to resolve the continuing conflict with the Zapatista rebels in the state of Chiapas. The new commission, which would include seven legislators representing the four major parties, promised to carry out the new president's earlier campaign commitment to use negotiations to settle the uprising, which had festered throughout 1994, and to move on to other items on his agenda.

Relations between the previous government, of Carlos Salinas de Gortari (1988–1994), and the Bush and Clinton administrations had been widely viewed as exemplary. Their teamwork in winning approval for NAFTA in late 1993 and for agreements on other bilateral issues was characterized as the most positive working atmosphere between the two neighbors in decades. The Bush administration had been instrumental in fashioning the so-called Brady Plan for renegotiating Mexico's foreign debt in the late 1980s, which opened the door to dramatic economic and financial reforms in Mexico; the Clinton administration had worked closely with the Salinas team in devising the strategy that resulted in relatively expeditious approval of NAFTA by the three signatories: Mexico, the United States, and Canada.

In this atmosphere of general optimism about the Mexican scene, there was little immediate response from official Washington after the December 20, 1995, devaluation. It was Christmas season, Congress was in recess, Treasury Secretary Lloyd Bentsen had resigned, and his replacement, Robert E. Rubin, had not yet taken office. But the White House began to feel intense pressure from a traumatized financial community within days of the decision. The mood in Washington did not improve after Serra Puche's feckless appearance later in the month at the New York Federal Reserve Bank, where he failed to convince some seventy top money managers and banking executives to remain confident about Mexico—and to stay invested.

As the deteriorating financial situation gathered mounting political significance for the Clinton administration, the first reaction at the White House to the devaluation was in terms of domestic politics. The president had staked a great deal, politically, on his activism on behalf of NAFTA. Now, with the devaluation, his worst fears were apparently about to be realized.

The event sustained the prophesy of one of NAFTA's most vocal critics, former presidential contender Ross Perot, who in testimony before a House panel on March 24, 1993, had warned, "These guys are just playing poker with us, and they are going to have to devalue the peso."[2] At the time, Perot had called for a companion agreement to the trade accord that would limit fluctuations in the peso, an idea the Bush and Clinton administrations never accepted. But, during his presidential campaign, Perot continued to maintain that the Mexican government would devalue the peso by 20 percent to 30 percent in 1994 and unleash a flood of low-priced goods on the U.S. market once trade barriers had been removed.

Before year's end the administration was facing the reality that the devaluation would in fact favor Mexican imports to the United States and stem the flow of U.S. products to Mexico. Worse still, instead of realizing NAFTA's promise of creating new U.S. jobs to service Mexican consumer demands, U.S. workers would see a loss of jobs as exports fell. The political ramifications for Clinton, particularly in those states likely to witness the job losses, could be very serious indeed by the time the 1996 presidential campaign rolled around.

The White House was also fully aware that a significant number of congressional Democrats had voted against NAFTA and that a number of consumer advocacy groups had also opposed the agreement. Consumer activist Ralph Nader lost no time in commenting on the devaluation and the likely need for a U.S. response, saying, "NAFTA was supposed to be about two-way trade not U.S. taxpayer welfare to prop up the Mexican peso and the Mexican oligarchs."[3]

The Clinton Administration Responds

See the need it did, but the White House moved cautiously in exploring ways of lending support to the Mexican monetary system. Not until the last days of December did the administration admit that it was considering a multibillion-dollar international aid package for Mexico. And only after President Zedillo announced an eagerly awaited emergency economic program on January 3, 1995 (which failed to reassure the markets), did the White House publicly offer support for restoring stability in Mexico.

In early January it was announced that the United States had agreed to pay for half of a U.S.$18 billion international loan package. The White House had decided to expand a permanent $6 billion credit line to $9 billion, with one-half coming from the treasury department's Exchange Stabilization Fund and the other half from the Federal Reserve System. Canada agreed to increase its standing credit line of Can.$1 billion to Can.$1.5 billion. The Bank for International Settlements (BIS) in Switzerland, a clearinghouse for European central banks, provided a commitment of U.S.$5 billion. A group of about a dozen international commercial banks had been asked to put up a U.S.$3 billion line of credit, but that initiative died a quiet death in the weeks following the announcement.

A few days later, Mexico asked the International Monetary Fund (IMF) for a new loan that effectively added U.S.$2.5 billion to $3.5 billion to the country's monetary reserves. The IMF made the loan available on a standby basis, allowing Mexico to draw it down as needed.

Three weeks after the devaluation, the Clinton administration refused to discuss the particulars of the crisis publicly. It was clear to the White House that additional aid was going to require congressional approval, and the new Republican majorities in both houses were suspicious of foreign aid generally. But a growing sense of impending doom in the markets finally flushed out the reluctant president, who commented: "We have a strong interest in prosperity and stability in Mexico. What we have is a short-term liquidity crisis. There was inevitably going to be some correction in the Mexican currency value because they had run a rather high budget deficit."[4]

The reaction by the Republican leadership to the president's announcement on January 18 of a loan guarantee package was initially, and unexpectedly, positive. The White House would describe this concurrence as a significant display of the ability to achieve bipartisanship in a foreign financial crisis. What the new speaker of the House, Newt Gingrich, and the new Senate majority leader, Robert Dole, agreed to was a rescue plan that would require Mexico to pay a fee, similar to an insurance premium, for the U.S. government's assuming the risk of guaranteeing Mexico's debts. The plan was said to avoid a potentially raucous congressional argument over foreign aid by allowing the legislative branch to approve the guarantees without having to allocate funds from the federal budget.

The announcement came after it had become clear to the White House that the $18 billion credit line for Mexico, created the previous week, was insufficient to stem the crisis. And in an orchestrated response, the Mexican government stated that the new package—the size of which was yet to be determined—would not cost U.S. taxpayers anything because Mexico would pay all the fees involved.

The Opposition in Washington Emerges

Within twenty-four hours of the bipartisan announcement of the loan guarantee package, the opposition began to assemble. Both the Republican leadership and the White House had known that rank-and-file members of both parties had become less enthusiastic about U.S. assistance to foreign countries since the end of the Cold War. Liberal Democrats with close ties to organized labor, as well as Republicans who relied on support from Perot admirers, were clearly nervous about giving their backing to the package.

Freshman senator Barbara Boxer (D.-Calif.), who had voted against NAFTA, said that the pending legislation would provide an opportunity for

Congress to reassess U.S. participation in NAFTA. And a group of fifteen representatives who had opposed the original pact went so far as to say they would try to force a U.S. withdrawal from the agreement.

If NAFTA was a constant and primary source of concern, illegal immigration ran a close second in terms of policy importance. In mid-January, the administration told congressional leaders that the number of illegal immigrants crossing the border into Texas and California would increase by 430,000 in 1995 if the Mexican financial crisis deepened. That estimate implied a 30 percent increase over earlier projections; Mexican workers were expected to be drawn to a dollar that had suddenly become 35 percent more valuable relative to the peso than before the December devaluation.

Even worse for the White House, Senator Dole appeared to be distancing himself from the package he had originally endorsed. The Senate majority leader said the president should not depend on Republicans to pass legislation authorizing the "bailout" unless he could bring along the Democrats. "He needs to work within his party," Dole stated. "We're not going to carry the whole load here and get hung out to dry."[5] If gloom characterized the White House that day, it deepened when the Democratic whip in the House, David Bonior of Michigan, vouched that "we must not be sending money to Mexico just to prop up a nation with the fastest-growing number of billionaires in the world."[6]

Even as Treasury Secretary Rubin and Federal Reserve Chairman Alan Greenspan were lobbying Congress on behalf of the loan guarantee package, support for it appeared to be crumbling. More and more members of Congress were demanding that special conditions be attached to the package—now set at $40 billion. Senator Jesse Helms, chairman of the Senate Foreign Relations Committee, pledged that in exchange for approving the guarantees he would "insist that Mexico make it a criminal act to try to leave the country without the necessary papers."[7] More moderate Republican senators also expressed doubts about the deal. And a growing number of Democrats in both houses, especially Class of 1992 survivors reelected in 1994, viewed the package as a bailout.

The bailout theme quickly became a rallying cry for the aggressive Republican freshmen in the House of Representatives. One group of them sent Speaker Gingrich a letter saying that the United States had no business bailing out a sovereign country. First-term member of Congress Steve Stockman (R.-Tex.) stated: "It's a bad deal for the United States, and it is a bad deal for the American people. What will be next, bailing out Orange County?"[8] Another letter that circulated among the House freshmen declared: "We are opposed to this proposal because we were elected to Congress to clear up the mess in Washington, not to approve a handout to the international financial community. We need to focus our energies on passing the Contract with America."[9]

When the White House came to believe that it was losing the battle for the loan guarantee package, the president for the first time made a direct public appeal to keep Mexico afloat. Speaking to a group of business leaders in mid-January, Clinton warned that Mexico's economic problems were "plainly also a danger to the economic future of the United States."[10] In the same meeting, also for the first time, Clinton said that he was acting partly out of a concern that Mexico's financial crisis could spread to other economies on which the United States was increasingly dependent: "If we fail to act, the crisis of confidence in Mexico's economy could spread to other emerging countries in Latin America and Asia, the kinds of markets that buy our goods and services today and that will buy far more of them in the future."[11]

Despite Clinton's protestations, the administration became less and less in control of the situation. The bipartisan framework of some weeks earlier had already begun to fray. Speaker Gingrich accused Pennsylvania Avenue of failing to get its forces organized behind the rescue plan, stating: "Opposition to it appears to be growing, particularly among the Democrats, which will frankly make it much harder to get Republicans. . . . It's not our fault that this administration does not seem to be able to get its ducks in a row. . . . I'm not holding [the aid package] hostage. . . . It will pass if they can get half the Democrats [to support it]."[12]

By late January, the administration was increasingly invoking national security, not just economic arguments, as justification for the package. But by then its "sell" was uphill. In the last week of January, the public's attention turned to a series of congressional hearings in which officials from both the administration and the Federal Reserve summarized the case in favor of the package. Secretary of State Warren Christopher testified before the House Banking and Financial Services Committee on January 25, pointing out that the United States had an immense economic and political stake in Mexico's stability. The secretary also stated that "approval of this loan guarantee package will have far-reaching implications for the prosperity and stability of Latin America and of emerging market economies around the world."[13] But most important, he said, was that "this is a test of American leadership."[14] Treasury Secretary Rubin, appearing before the same committee, made the argument that "the risks are not only in Mexico. Restoring confidence in Mexico will head off the spread of financial distress around the world. The fastest-growing customers for U.S. products are the most likely to feel the financial spillover from problems in Mexico. U.S.-manufactured exports to developing countries expanded by 65 percent between 1989 and 1993; more than two-fifths of our overall exports are now destined for these countries. These are countries with great potential, countries where U.S. investors have large stakes."[15] And in an appearance before the Senate Foreign Relations Committee on January 26, Fed Chairman Greenspan argued: "The objective of the proposed guarantee program is to halt the erosion in Mexico's financing capabilities before it has dramatic impacts far beyond those already evident around the world. This program in my judgment is the least worst of the various initiatives which present themselves as possible solutions to a very unsettling international financial problem."[16]

In what might have been a timely and influential endorsement of Mexico's stabilization program, the IMF agreed on January 27, 1995, to lend Mexico U.S.$7.58 billion, the largest loan in the fund's fifty-year history. Recently appointed Mexican finance minister Guillermo Ortiz stated that the monies would be added to the reserves of the central bank for the nation's various payment needs. But on the night of January 31, the White House abruptly decided to withdraw the proposed loan guarantee program from Congress. Abandoning the $40 billion package, the president decided to use his own emergency authority to loan up to $20 billion to Mexico to prevent its defaulting on government-issued bonds. The new package— $11 billion larger than the original proposal—required no congressional approval. In an official statement, the president indicated that the overall package would include $20 billion from the Exchange Stabilization Fund, $17.8 billion from the IMF, and $10 billion from the Bank for International Settlement. And in a joint statement, President Clinton, Speaker Gingrich, House minority leader Richard Gephardt (D.-Mo.), majority leader Dole, and Senate minority leader Thomas Daschle (D.-S.D.) stated: "We must act now in order to protect American jobs, prevent an increased flow of illegal immigrants across our borders, ensure stability in this hemisphere, and encourage reform in emerging markets around the world. . . . This is an important undertaking, and we believe that the risks of inaction vastly exceed any risks associated with this action. We fully support this effort, and we will work to ensure that its purposes are met. . . . We have agreed to act today."[17]

And so the Clinton administration's efforts to organize a congressionally approved loan guarantee package for Mexico had failed. Despite the efforts of the Federal Reserve, of some congressional leaders, and of the White House itself, the Congress as a whole appeared increasingly resistant, and some of its members were even adamantly opposed, to accepting the administration's arguments on either domestic or national security grounds. Why?

The Many Arguments Against the First Rescue Package

It is clear that the first rescue package, announced on January 12, reawakened the deep-seated opposition to NAFTA that had lingered not only along the Potomac but across the country. Opponents of the agreement, on the left and the right, saw the package as just another scheme to reward the rich and ignore the poor—in both the United States and Mexico. Democrats still resented the fact that, despite subsequent side agreements on the environment and labor, their concerns in these areas had been overlooked in the final NAFTA language. Conservatives were anxious to avoid being seen as advocates of a trade agreement that Ross Perot had condemned as unfair to this country.

But there were even stronger currents at work in Washington in early 1995 that would doom the loan guarantee package. With hindsight we can see that the bipartisan leadership's early support for the program had failed to take into account the arrival not just of new majorities in both houses of the Congress but also of dozens and dozens of new senators and representatives. Many of the new legislators had not expected to be elected; they had run as underdogs and wound up defeating long-seated, senior Democratic incumbents. Most had run as fiscal conservatives and were strong and enthusiastic supporters of the new speaker's "Contract with America." These freshmen believed that U.S. voters had given them a mandate to pursue, and they had a hundred days in which to respond. The contract's particulars focused on domestic issues; there was little room for—or interest in—foreign affairs, among either the 1994 newcomers or the populist survivors from the Democratic Party's freshman class of 1992.

As Republican leaders were beginning to grasp these new realities, they also started to sense a reprise of the schisms in the Democratic Party over the NAFTA vote in 1993. Minority leader Gephardt in the House was, at best, lukewarm toward the package. Congressman Bonior, the third-ranking member of the Democratic leadership after Daschle and Gephardt, was publicly hostile to the arrangement. Anti-NAFTA members of Congress signed on quickly to oppose the package. Lobbying with the opposition were consumer, labor, and environmental advocates, who saw a vote against the loan guarantees as a vote against NAFTA and the Mexican regime.

The administration had thought the time-honored call to duty to support the president in a time of crisis would be persuasive. It was not. Congress rejected with impunity the calls for U.S. leadership, the defense of U.S. national security interests, and related goals. The Cold War was over. The new majority in Congress had a domestic agenda and little time in which to address it. Foreign aid, bailouts, and other forms of support for developing countries had little resonance in the Capital.

The congressional rebuff of the call to support the president raises a number of issues for the future. Was the administration's inability to summon legislative support simply a reflection of a weakened Clinton presidency? Or did it portend greater autonomy for the legislature and a less powerful role for the chief executive in matters of foreign affairs? Is the Mexican crisis the opening of a new chapter in congressional-presidential relations in the foreign policy arena or an aberration that reflected momentary isolationism on the part of a new Republican—and conservative—Congress?

The old populist arguments against helping Wall Street and billionaires, here or there, were persuasive for many members in both houses. And presidential politics entered the debate when Senator Dole distanced himself from a program that was unpopular with the U.S. public generally and with key members of Congress from states that he would need to win the Republican nomination in 1996. Dole's shift in position was clearly a response to the unrelenting criticism of the package by Senator Phil Gramm (R.-Tex.), a major contender for the Republican nomination and to the right, politically, of Dole.

On the other side of the aisle not only were the Democrats divided, but they received little support from the White House other than the rhetoric of presidential statements or testimony by leading advocates in the administration. Democrats easily saw the political downside of a vote in favor of the package; but few articulated—or were provided—a compelling case for the upside, other than patriotism and national security. The unpopular president had few arrows in his quiver.

Round one, then, was both a tactical and a strategic failure for the Clinton administration. In turning to a second option, the White House would find that the opposition did not end on February 1 and that the same dynamics that had defeated Bill Clinton's efforts to win congressional support for the $40 billion program would haunt his efforts to implement and sustain minimal political support for the second effort.

The February Package

With relief the congressional leadership welcomed the president's decision to withdraw the $40 billion program. But the GOP freshmen, disregarding their leaders, continued their attack against the second package. They argued that the president had unfairly circumvented Congress, that he had not imposed adequate conditions on Mexico, that hearings should be called to explore the subject, and that the administration could and should have reacted more swiftly to Mexico's economic crisis in 1994.

In spite of these criticisms, consultations between the leadership on Capitol Hill and the White House proceeded relatively smoothly during February 1995. On February 21, the basic accord between the two countries was signed in Washington by secretaries Rubin and Ortiz. President Clinton praised Mexico's leaders for taking "some very courageous steps" and asserted that the deal was not a bailout. "We have very good collateral on this deal," he stated, a reference to the U.S. requirements that all of

Mexico's export earnings on oil be available to back the loans. "So we have done the right thing by the American taxpayers and the American people as well," Clinton concluded.[18]

But toward the end of February, a disturbing policy issue arose. Was Mexico unique? If Mexico's ills spread, was Washington prepared to bail out other emerging markets that were trading partners? The administration waffled. Senior officials were reluctant to say yes or no. But the question is significant. *Are* there other countries—such as Brazil and Argentina—so vital to U.S. interests that similar action would need to be taken in the future? There is still no clear answer to this troubling question.

Still other critics echoed the harsh question raised by Michael Prowse in the *New Republic:* whether global investors "are to be treated as adults or children."

> Are they to be responsible or not? We are supposedly entering a brave new world of global capitalism. Economic development is being powered by market forces, rather than the financial largess of finance ministers and multilateral agencies such as the IMF and the World Bank. . . .
>
> Countries have to pay a price for imprudent policies; individuals have to pay a price for rash investments. The problem with bailouts is that they reward irresponsibility and so make future crises more likely. Rubin & Co. wanted to make global capitalism safe for the mutual fund investor. They actually made it far riskier.[19]

During the first week in March, policymakers in Washington and Mexico City had to go further on the defensive. The peso had fallen to a record low against the dollar, as financial markets reacted to the Mexican government's delay in announcing policies to deal with the rapid deterioration of the economy. IMF officials flew to Mexico City to hold talks with the government on how to adjust the country's economic program to cope with the continuing weakness of the peso. In Washington, Lawrence Summers, undersecretary of the treasury, said it was clear that economic forecasts made at the time the agreements were first negotiated would have to be revised, but he expected Mexico to live up to its policy commitments to control the growth of credit, maintain budget discipline, and continue with the process of privatization.[20]

Republicans and Democrats in Congress continued to attack U.S. policy toward Mexico, calling on the administration not to give any more money. On March 9, in the nick of time, the Mexican government announced a new austerity program, which was quickly hailed by the White House as the right medicine and endorsed by the IMF. Finance Minister Ortiz visited Wall Street on March 14 armed with flip charts, color slides, and infinite patience to answer investor questions.

But in an ominous sign for the U.S. economy and the Clinton administration, the Commerce Department reported in late March that the U.S.

trade deficit had soared by two-thirds in the year ending January 31, 1995, to a record $12.23 billion. There was strong evidence that the usual imbalance, caused largely by Asian imports that far exceed U.S. exports to the region, was worsening as Mexico plunged deeper into economic crisis. The White House was particularly concerned, because a further deterioration in trade could keep the dollar weak. And if the economy were to slow, as expected, later in 1995, the Republicans would have the ammunition to attack what otherwise has been Clinton's strong suit—the healthy U.S. economy.

More ominous were the trade data for March, which indicated that the critic's prediction of a fallout from the peso collapse was already coming to pass. Mexico, which in recent years had helped counterbalance the chronic U.S. trade deficit with Asia, was now beginning to help widen the gap. The March numbers were expected to be the first in a long series of Mexican trade surpluses with the United States, as the steep devaluation continued to hurt America's third-largest export market.

Even before the trade imbalances were announced, the Republican majority in Congress moved to limit the chief executive's freedom of action in setting U.S. policy toward Mexico. On March 1, the House passed a resolution of inquiry requesting detailed documentation about the aid package. On March 16, the Senate adopted an amendment to the emergency supplemental defense appropriations bill to require the administration to certify that the United States would not incur costs for any loan or guarantee extended to Mexico. Offered by Senator Hank Brown (R.-Colo.), the Mexican Debt Disclosure Act would require the president to certify— before any loan, guarantee, or swap can be made—that there is no projected cost to the United States; that all loans, credits, guarantees, and swaps are adequately collateralized to ensure that U.S. financing will be repaid; that the Mexican government has made effective efforts to establish an independent central bank or currency control mechanism; and that Mexico has a significant economic reform effort in effect.

On March 22, the Senate Foreign Relations Committee approved a resolution calling on the administration to provide detailed monthly reports on Mexico and to certify that the United States will not incur costs for any loan or guarantee extended to that country. And in approving the resolution, which encompassed Senator Brown's Mexican Debt Disclosure Act, the committee also attached an amendment by its chair, Senator Jesse Helms (R.-N.C.), requiring the president to make available to Congress information on any involvement in drug trafficking by senior Mexican government officials since 1991. The president signed the Mexican Debt Disclosure Act on April 10, 1995.

Surprising the administration, Senator Alfonse D'Amato (R.-N.Y.) and a group of Republican supporters stalled a vote on a Senate budget-cutting bill by introducing an amendment aimed at blocking the loan package to

Mexico. And in early May, House Speaker Gingrich accused the administration of violating federal law by continuing to provide aid to Mexico
even though the White House had failed to make available to Congress
documents required by law. Writing to the president on May 4, Gingrich
expressed "serious concern" that the administration had violated the Mexican Debt Disclosure Act: "Your violation of the act's disclosure requirements means that the administration's current expenditures on the Mexican
assistance program . . . are a direct violation of federal law. . . . The administration must bear full responsibility for this situation and its consequences, which could easily have been avoided. . . . I fully expect that this
violation of law will be immediately rectified."[21]

Criticism of the aid package continued through the summer of 1995.
In a Senate hearing on July 14 convened by the Senate Banking Committee, Chairman D'Amato attacked the administration for releasing to Mexico an additional $2.5 billion in loans in July—for a total of $12.5 billion
disbursed. Responding for the administration, Treasury Secretary Rubin
defended the administration's arrangements and stated that the "potential
escalation of the crisis in Mexico was a direct, long-term threat to American and national security interests" in the form of illegal immigration and
restricted trade flows.[22]

In late July, in protest against the financial rescue plan, the House
voted 254 to 193 to curb future use of the Treasury's Exchange Stabilization Fund for "the purpose of bolstering any foreign currency." While the
House language did not become law, it clearly indicated the strong opposition in the Congress to any further support for Mexico.[23]

The pessimism in Washington, and on Wall Street, was not helped
when, in mid-August, finance minister Guillermo Ortiz announced that the
Mexican economy had contracted by 10.5 percent in the second quarter of
1995, the worst decline in more than a decade. Reactions were swift and
troubled. Many pointed to the overall fragility of the Mexican economy,
while others raised questions about the ability of the government to stage
an economic recovery in the near future. There were calls for a new set of
policies to reverse the depth of the economic slump as well as the appreciation of the peso. The gloomy news about the recession in Mexico was
deepened by a report published by the International Monetary Fund in late
August, which cited "information asymmetry" in Mexico and other emerging markets as a key reason for the investor nervousness that had sparked
December's peso crisis. The IMF report suggested that a greater sharing of
financial data by the Mexican government with both domestic and foreign
investors could have stemmed an outward flood of capital in early December or, at a minimum, would have helped investors make more informed decisions.

President Ernesto Zedillo's September 1 state-of-the-union speech was
received with cautious optimism. In the address, he promised to increase

spending to stimulate the economy in the last five months of 1995. The spending program, the government believed, would move Mexico again toward growth. But Finance Minister Ortiz ran into skepticism when he visited Wall Street in late September. As one fund manager commented, "He told us a good story, but the story isn't making people feel they need to run out and buy Mexican equities."[24] The skepticism of many on Wall Street was reenforced in late September with the release of an Organization for Economic Cooperation and Development (OECD) survey on Mexico that urged the country to maintain fiscal austerity and a floating exchange rate for several years. Contrary to government forecasts, the OECD stated that Mexico's recovery "would be a more protracted process," largely because households and companies were too deeply in debt and the privatized banking system had been weakened by bad loans.[25]

In preparation for a state visit by Zedillo to the United States in mid-October, the government announced an early repayment of $700 million of the $12.5 billion it had borrowed earlier in the year. The gesture was viewed as being as much a political payback as an economic one. The repayment provided the Clinton administration with ammunition to argue that his decision earlier in the year to support Mexico had been correct. But the positive fallout from the early payback was quickly offset by two political events. The first was the resignation from the Institutional Revolutionary Party (PRI) of Manuel Camacho, former foreign minister, Chiapas peace negotiator, and once thought to be the most likely 1994 presidential candidate. The resignation of the prominent and politically savvy Camacho was paralleled by a bold military display by the Zapatista National Liberation Army in Chiapas on the eve of the first substantive negotiations between the Mexican government and the guerrillas.

October ended with the beginning of a crisis of confidence in the peso that had not abated by year-end. The peso plummeted to a seven-month low, accompanied by a serious two-day dip in the stock market. The peso, which had been steadily sliding in value in the previous two months, sank below the psychological threshold of seven to the dollar. The drop of more than 5 percent in the peso's value was the worst single-day fall since Zedillo's mid-March stabilization plan was announced. Analysts said the peso's plunge was indicative of overall market uncertainty about Mexico's economic condition and investor fears that harsh austerity measures imposed by the IMF were failing to rein in the economy. Most alarming was a government announcement that inflation for the first two weeks of October totaled 1.1 percent—an alarmingly high figure for such a short period.

November 1995 saw a number of positive and negative developments in Mexico. The peso began a week-long process of high volatility in early November as confidence in the economic outlook continued to deteriorate. The government announced the Alliance for Economic Recovery, which was a wage, price, and tax agreement between the government and trade union and business leaders. *Pactos,* as these agreements are known in Spanish, were an integral part of the planning process after the first was negotiated in 1987. The old *pactos* were an integral part of the heterodox approach to economic policy in the Salinas administration, which combined orthodox fiscal and monetary measures with agreed measures to limit price and wage rises. But the Zedillo government has had to abandon that approach since the devaluation. This is in large part because the government lost the hinge of the previous accords: the pre-set maximum rate of depreciation of the peso. The government, in announcing the agreement, reaffirmed that a floating peso would be maintained, and cited no targets. While welcomed, the agreement did not have a major impact on the markets.

Zedillo also announced a major reorganization of the country's fifty-two-year-old social security system, with the goal of improving medical services and increasing the sagging rate of domestic savings. The proposal by the government opened a political debate about changing a program that had become one of the major "birthrights" of the average Mexican. The social security reform measures were announced as data released by the government showed that gross domestic product (GDP) fell 9.6 percent in the third quarter from the same period in 1994. This followed a 10.5 percent decline in the second quarter.

The uncertainty surrounding the future of the economy was further complicated in November with the revelation that Carlos Salinas's sister-in-law, the wife of Raúl Salinas, had been arrested in Switzerland after trying to make a large withdrawal from a Swiss bank account using a fraudulent power of attorney. The money was in three bank accounts bearing a fictitious name. At the end of November, it was announced that the Mexican congress had voted to set up a commission of inquiry to investigate the rapid enrichment of Raúl Salinas. This was the first time the legislature had decided to investigate a senior political figure. As the year ended, former president Carlos Salinas, in self-imposed exile, accused groups in Mexico of attempting to smear his reputation and offered to defend himself against all accusations.

Conclusions

Throughout the events of the last quarter of 1995, in comparison to the first months of the year, the Clinton administration was eerily quiet about Mexico. While there were intermittent negative comments from members of Congress, the administration refused to be pushed into either a confrontation or a statement of renewed concern for the future of the Mexican economy. Commentators indicated that the presidential campaign was one reason; another reason, of course, was that there was little the United

States could do for Mexico other than to continue to accept Mexican exports. Additional financial support was out of the question, given the opposition in Congress. The future of NAFTA remained up in the air. It was clear that the president would not receive fast-track authorization to open negotiations for the expansion of the trade pact to include Chile prior to the November 1996 presidential elections. Immigration and drugs continued to preoccupy specialists in the government but, tacitly, it was understood that neither issue could be addressed seriously until a modicum of economic stability was evident in Mexico and the electoral process in the United States had finished.

The aftermath of the December 1994 devaluation continued to be felt throughout 1995 and apparently is continuing to play a negative role in 1996 as many doubt the numbers offered by Mexican authorities about inflation levels, the value of the peso, interest rates, and related topics of keen interest to the investor community and to the international financial institutions. As one observer wrote in mid-December: "Central bankers have a saying that 'confidence is always rented, never owned.' Mexico rented a lot of confidence in the early 1990s and lost it all last year, and is now discovering how hard it is to win back. Mexico's biggest problem today is that global investors . . . have too many other good choices where to put their money."[26]

Washington continued to remain mute through the year-end with regard to the future of the Mexican economy, the scandals, political reform, and the continuing saga of who committed the assassinations of the prominent Mexicans who died in 1993 and 1994. As the U.S. electoral campaign looms larger and larger in the thinking of the White House, it is unlikely that 1996 will see any change in policy. That leaves the optimists to believe that the corner has been turned and growth will be resumed; the pessimists, in alarm, wait for the next fault line to appear—economic or political—with little sense of whether policymakers in Mexico or in the United States will know how to respond and whether the longer-term implications of not responding are well understood in the United States.

Notes

1. Craig Torres, "Mexico's Goal for '95 Growth May Be Tough," *Wall Street Journal,* December 16, 1994, p. A8.

2. Keith Bradsher, "Political Perils Showing in Free Trade Accord," *New York Times,* December 23, 1994, p. D4.

3. Ibid.

4. Ted Bardacke, "Clinton Ready to Enlarge Mexico's $9 Bn Credit Line," *Financial Times,* January 12, 1995, p. 1.

5. David E. Sanger, "Mexico Crisis Seen Spurring Flow of Aliens," *New York Times,* January 18, 1995, p. A1.

6. Ibid.

7. George Graham, "U.S. Congress Warned on Mexico Pledge," *Financial Times,* January 18, 1995, p. 6.

8. "New Republicans, Old NAFTA Foe Oppose Mexico Aid," *Reuters,* January 18, 1995.

9. "Mexican Aid Knocked by Freshmen in Congress," *Telerrate,* January 18, 1995.

10. David E. Sanger, "With Opposition Rising, Clinton Pleads for Mexico Rescue Package," *New York Times,* January 19, 1995, p. A21.

11. Ibid.

12. "Mexico Aid Package Troubled," *Reuters,* January 20, 1995.

13. U.S. House of Representatives, Banking and Financial Services Committee, testimony, Secretary of State Warren Christopher, January 25, 1995, Washington, D.C.: Federal Document Clearinghouse, 1995.

14. Ibid.

15. U.S. House of Representatives, Banking and Financial Services Committee, testimony, Secretary of the Treasury Robert L. Rubin, January 25, 1995, Washington, D.C.: Federal Document Clearinghouse, 1995.

16. Testimony of Alan Greenspan, chairman, Board of Governors of the Federal Reserve System, before the Committee on Foreign Relations, U.S. Senate, January 26, 1995.

17. White House, Office of Public Liaison, January 31, 1995, photocopy.

18. David E. Sanger, "Limits on Mexico," *New York Times,* February 22, 1995, p. A1.

19. Michael Prowse, "The Rescuers," *New Republic,* February 27, 1995, pp. 11–12.

20. Leslie Crawford, "IMF Talks on Mexico Programme: Peso's Steady Slide Means Economic Targets Must Be Renegotiated," *Financial Times,* March 8, 1995, p. 6.

21. Keith Bradsher, "Mexican Bailout Defended Amid G.O.P. Criticism," *Washington Post,* July 15, 1995, p. D1.

22. Ibid.

23. David Wessel, "House, Protesting Bailout of Mexico, Votes to Limit Use of Treasury Fund," *Wall Street Journal,* July 20, 1995, p. 18.

24. Peter Truell, "Mexico Makes a Pitch, but Wall Street Is Wary," *New York Times,* September 19, 1995, p. D3.

25. Leslie Crawford, "Austerity Urged on Mexico," *Financial Times,* September 27, 1995, p. 6.

26. Thomas L. Friedman, "The Coffin's Free," *New York Times,* December 13, 1995, p. A23.

4

Recent Economic Policy in Brazil Before and After the Mexican Peso Crisis

Celso L. Martone

The collapse of the Mexican peso in December 1994 produced, although for the most part temporarily, economic and policy repercussions in Brazil. At a deeper level, it raised some fundamental questions about the two most praised economic policy models in Latin America in the 1990s: the exchange rate–based model of monetary stabilization and the so-called neoliberal model of economic development. In my view, the economic and political consequences of the Mexican experience (and of the more recent Argentine and Brazilian experiences) have not been fully understood. This chapter develops some preliminary analysis of the impact of the Mexican devaluation on Brazil's economy and economic policy. To do that, it is necessary first to describe developments in Brazil leading to the *Real* Plan of July 1994, inspired by events in Mexico and Argentina, as well as to review the advances made in the area of structural reforms and economic liberalization.

Brazil has been lagging behind other major countries in Latin America in terms of both monetary stabilization and economic liberalization. At least five major stabilization plans launched in 1991, based on general price freezes, did not last more than a few months, leading to four-digit inflation for most of the period. A serious policy to open the trade system, to deregulate the economy, and to privatize part of the gigantic public sector started only in 1990, under the Collor administration, and was soon interrupted by the president's ouster in October 1992. In July 1994, the conditions were finally in place for the implementation of a new stabilization plan similar to the ones applied in Mexico and Argentina. This chapter describes the implementation of the plan and concentrates on the analysis of the policies required to sustain the relative monetary stability achieved in the past eighteen months and to create a favorable environment for growth.

The first section discusses the main interpretations of the Mexican crisis as seen from the Brazilian perspective. The second section reviews the recent economic developments in Brazil to December 1994, covering the first six months of the *Real* Plan. The contagion effect of the Mexican devaluation and the policy responses of the Cardoso administration are presented in the third section. In the fourth section, I argue that a serious trade-off between inflation and growth exists today, and that the only possible way to sustain low inflation and high growth in the coming years is to abandon the exchange rate anchor and at the same time promote decisive progress in the economic reform process, especially in the area of fiscal reforms. The timid and compromising proposals for fiscal reform of the Cardoso administration, and the resistance of the congress to approve them, are producing a dangerous time mismatch between the requirements of the stabilization policy and the pace of the reforms to sustain it. The fifth section concludes with some conjectures for the future.

Brazilian Interpretations of the Mexican Financial Collapse

The December 1994 devaluation of the Mexican peso and its still unfolding economic consequences have been interpreted in Brazil from three distinct but not mutually exclusive points of view: as a failure of economic policy, as the sudden and perhaps premature end of an unsustainable credit cycle, and as a breakdown of the so-called neoliberal model of development. Let us examine each of these viewpoints in turn.

A Failed Economic Policy?

As a matter of economic policy, the Mexican devaluation represented strong if not conclusive evidence against what is known as the exchange rate–based model of economic stabilization—a model highly fashionable in Latin America in the first half of the 1990s. The argument in favor of the model is that, in economies with chronically low credibility stemming from the historic instability of their monetary and fiscal regimes, the most effective and least costly way to achieve monetary stability is to link the domestic price level to the world price level through the fixity (or pegging) of the nominal exchange rate.

This model is called into use only when enough foreign capital is available to finance the country's temporary current-account deficits. The availability of foreign capital depends, in turn, on either a previous reserve accumulation (as in the recent case of Brazil) or an elastic supply of resources in the world capital markets. The international credit cycle of the late 1980s and early 1990s guaranteed the second scenario and made experimenting with the exchange rate model an attractive policy alternative in several Latin American countries, such as Mexico, Argentina, and Brazil.

From a theoretical standpoint, however, pegging the nominal exchange rate to the world price level is neither necessary nor sufficient for monetary stability. Permanent monetary stability requires a balanced government budget in the present value sense, a monetary rule imposed on the central bank consistent with price level stability, and strong foreign and domestic confidence in the nation's fiscal and monetary regimes. In countries suffering from chronic inflation, those conditions can be achieved only gradually and with great discipline, through an ongoing effort to reconstruct the fiscal and monetary institutions crippled by the inflation. Thus, pegging the nominal exchange rate is at best a temporary measure, one that lowers inflation while more fundamental changes are implemented.

Moreover, from a practical standpoint, pegging the nominal exchange rate to reduce inflation usually engenders for the real exchange rate a time path that is inconsistent with external market equilibrium. In other words, if the real exchange rate resulting from the temporary price stability leads to an unsustainably long period of foreign indebtedness, inflationary expectations will persist and credibility will not improve. Sooner or later a crisis of confidence develops, destroying monetary stability.

Notwithstanding these theoretical and practical considerations, two arguments have been developed to defend the model. The first is that any real appreciation of the currency that occurs after stabilization does not represent a permanent balance-of-payments problem because the price stability itself and concurrent domestic structural reforms (privatization, deregulation, and reforms of financial and trade policies) will increase the productivity of the domestic economy to an extent that it compensates for the lower real exchange rate. The second argument posits that even if an upward correction in the real exchange rate becomes necessary in the future, it can be effected without triggering inflation again, because the reformed monetary and fiscal systems will then be consistent with price stability. Thus, the pegged exchange rate serves as a temporary anchor for the economy, one that will be replaced by permanent fiscal and monetary anchors in due time.

Although these two arguments make sense in principle, the fact is that it has been extremely difficult to abandon the exchange rate anchor even after substantial progress in structural reforms has been made, as the experiences of Mexico and Argentina have shown. One reason seems to be that public confidence in the country's financial and monetary institutions does not seem to take hold, so that lifting the exchange rate anchor precipitates renewed inflationary expectations. Another reason is associated with the relative price effect of a real devaluation. A real devaluation leads to a reallocation of resources from the nontradable sector to the tradable sector of the economy, producing not only frictions in the markets but also, in most cases, temporary recession and higher unemployment. Finally, after the private and the public sectors have engaged in heavy foreign borrowing at an overvalued exchange rate, a real devaluation will have devastating effects on the financial structure and solvency of both firms and the government. It should be recalled that most governments in Latin America assumed a large part of the private foreign debt during the 1982 debt crisis to prevent widespread bankruptcies. For all these and possibly other reasons, the governments have tended to maintain the exchange rate anchor longer than they expected and longer than is tenable.

An Unsustainable Credit Cycle?

The second main interpretation of the Mexican crisis as viewed from Brazil stresses the dependency of Latin America's economies on the international credit cycle and especially on the cycle of the U.S. economy. It seems that when international conditions are favorable, the region tends to embark on a path of foreign indebtedness that is simply unsustainable over the longer term. Indeed, Latin America's debt accumulation of the 1990s is not qualitatively different from the previous cycle of the 1970s that culminated in the debt crisis of 1982. That crisis took almost a decade to overcome, only to be followed by renewed borrowing.

Some basic statistics help to illustrate the more recent cycle. In the period 1990–1994, Latin American economies as a whole grew, on average, 3.4 percent annually—a much better performance than in the 1980s, when international capital markets had been closed to the region. Average annual inflation dropped from some 1,200 percent in 1990 (100 percent if Brazil is excluded) to 465 percent in 1994 (16 percent if Brazil is excluded)—the lowest inflation in the region in some decades.[1]

At the same time, the trade balance of the region turned from a surplus of U.S.$27 billion in 1990 to a deficit of $18 billion in 1994, while the current-account balance deteriorated from an annual deficit of $4 billion to $50 billion and real effective exchange rates appreciated some 30 percent on the average during the period. With the region's total gross domestic product (GDP) approaching $1.2 trillion in 1994, the current-account deficit represented around 3.5 percent of GDP in that year—well above the 2 percent level conventionally assumed to be sustainable in the long run. The region's external indebtedness increased $86 billion, from $438 billion in 1990 to $524 billion in 1994. Net external financing was maintained at over $50 billion per year. A kind of Ponzi game by Latin American governments therefore seemed to be repeating itself in the early 1990s.[2]

These trends raise the question of the inadequacy of the average domestic savings rate in the region (under 20 percent of GDP) relative to the desired growth of consumption and its associated investment requirement. To be sustained in the medium term, high growth rates of consumption require investment rates well above domestic savings rates and unsustainable deficits in the current account. More than that, as the Mexican experience demonstrates, the capital inflows help finance domestic consumption and do not predominantly translate into higher investment rates. The particular challenge is to determine what can be done to increase domestic savings besides instituting high real interest rates, which is the traditional instrument used by governments to check consumption.

Financial liberalization, of both the domestic banking system and external capital movements, has also been questioned as premature, inadequate, or too risky. Liberalization was absolutely necessary, however, to gain access to world capital markets and to qualify as an "emerging market." During the 1970s, when most foreign loans were made by commercial banks and official financial institutions, there was no need for financial liberalization. On the contrary, the model of foreign lending of the 1970s coincided with the tightly closed foreign exchange regimes in most Latin American countries and with a large part of lending being done directly or guaranteed by the public sector. During the 1990s, by contrast, foreign funds have been channeled primarily through worldwide capital markets, with thousands of small, independent decisionmakers requiring freedom of capital movements.

A Breakdown of the Neoliberal Model?

Finally, from a political or ideological standpoint, Brazilian socialists, nationalists, and conservatives alike have interpreted the Mexican collapse as a failure of the "neoliberal" model of development so long preached by the International Monetary Fund (IMF) and the World Bank. According to this view, economic liberalization (again, privatization, deregulation, and reforms of financial and trade policies) and the concomitant downsizing of the state have simply been inadequate for the immature and fragile economic systems of the region. It is not yet clear whether and to what extent the Mexican crisis will lead to a reversal of liberalizing policies across the region, but it certainly is likely to contribute to a reining in of these policies.

Recent Economic Policies and Developments in Brazil, 1989–1994

As noted at the outset, Brazil has, since 1986, instituted a succession of more heterodox economic stabilization plans than the neoliberal project in Mexico: the Cruzado Plan (February 1986), the Bresser Plan (June 1987), the Verão (Summer) Plan (January 1989), the Collor I Plan (March 1990), the Collor II Plan (February 1991), and finally the *Real* Plan (July 1994). A principal argument for the Brazilian approach has been that the "magic" drop in inflation brought about by a general price freeze would create the political support necessary to undertake the structural reforms—especially fiscal reform—that would otherwise be impossible to imagine, given the country's fragmented political system and deeply entrenched interest groups within the government. The historical record of the past decade, however, shows the opposite result. After the Brazilian economy attained a period of temporary price stability, the political system merely accommodated itself to the new reality and actually became even more resistant to any kind of reform. Inflation eventually returned, the only possible outcome of the macroeconomic imbalances caused by the government's plan. Indeed, Brazil has been an example of successive attempts at monetary stabilization *without* structural reforms. Between 1986 and 1994, the Brazilian currency changed name five times (from cruzeiro to cruzado, then to cruzado novo, back to cruzeiro, then to cruzeiro real, and finally to *real*). Over the same period, the currency unit was cumulatively divided by 2.75 trillion. Figure 4.1 shows monthly changes in the dollar value of the currency and the inflation rate over the years 1989–1995.

The Brazilian public's opinion of the heterodox approach has gradually changed as a result of growing disillusionment with the populism and clientelism of the "new republic" and with economic stagnation, four-digit

Figure 4.1 Brazil's Monthly Exchange Rate Depreciation and Rate of Inflation, 1989–1995 (percent per month)

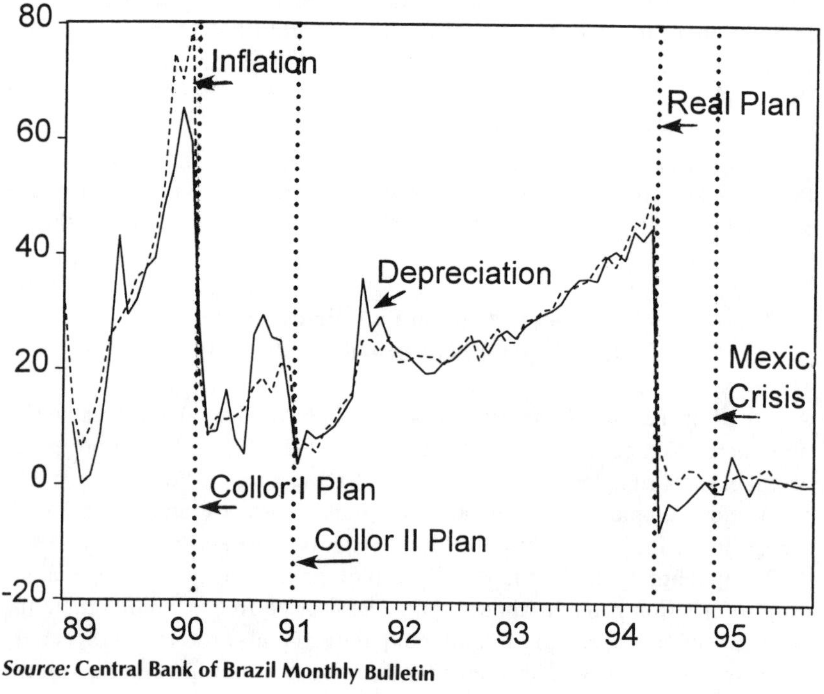

Source: Central Bank of Brazil Monthly Bulletin

inflation, and the benefits that seemed to be accruing from the neoliberal policies adopted in some other Latin American countries, especially Mexico and Argentina.

The Collor Administration, 1989–1992

The first political expression of the evolving public perceptions, and the first real challenge to the prevailing political and economic structures, was the victory in the 1989 presidential campaign of Fernando Collor de Mello's modernization platform: monetary stability, widespread deregulation of markets, downsizing of the state (through privatization and reform of the tax and social security systems), and liberalization of trade restrictions.

But the Collor administration made two fatal errors that led to its premature end in October 1992. The first was the so-called Collor Plan of monetary stabilization, launched in March 1990 on the heels of a hyperinflation. The plan was based on the mistaken notion that the inflationary process was being caused by a "monetary overhang," an excessive stock of liquid financial assets in the hands of the private sector, a large part of which was short-term government paper. To adjust the overstock, the plan imposed a capital levy of about one-third on the financial assets in question (also improperly called "indexed money") and extended their maturity to eighteen months. Figure 4.2 shows the results. An enormous liquidity squeeze developed, inflation dropped to zero instantly (see Figure 4.1), and a deep recession began. Alarmed by the recessionary effects of the plan, the government rapidly remonetized the economy. Ten months later, inflation was back at 20 percent per month, and a Collor II Plan had to be implemented in February 1991 (a new general price freeze) merely to regain some temporary control over the economy. The government never recovered from that fatal error of its macroeconomic policy, even after a radical shuffling of the finance ministry in May 1991.

The second mistake was a combination of profound neglect of the political forces in the congress and a massive corruption scheme extending through numerous arms of the government. When the scheme was uncovered and publicly denounced in May 1992, there were no political allies to support the government. An impeachment process was initiated, leading to the president's ouster in October to facilitate the investigations. In December, when the outcome of the process was already clear, the president resigned in order to avoid his formal impeachment.

Thus, Collor's economic and political failings retarded the structural reforms he had planned for Brazil. Inflation returned to the four-digit level in 1992. Between 1990 and 1992, real GDP decreased 4.2 percent, and industrial output fell 11.8 percent. The Collor administration did succeed, however, in instituting substantial trade liberalization and partial privatization of government-held industries (namely, steel and petrochemicals).

**Figure 4.2   Monthly Monetary Aggregates: Selected Measures of the Money
Supply in Brazil, 1989–1995 (in U.S.$ billions)**

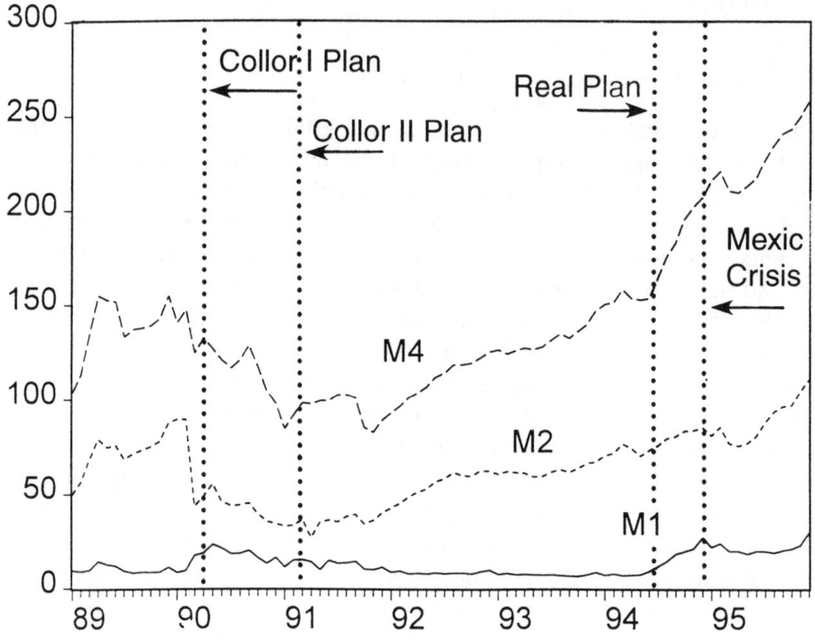

Source: Central Bank of Brazil Monthly Bulletin

The trade reform eliminated nontariff barriers to imports and reduced the average tariff from about 40 percent to 14 percent and the maximum tariff from 85 percent to 40 percent over a four-year period, which together have brought significant changes to the Brazilian industrial structure. Those structural reforms had their international effects as well: Brazil has since come to be recognized as an "emerging market" and has effectively gained access to world capital markets.

The Franco Administration, 1992–1994, and Cardoso's Real *Plan*

The succeeding presidential administration, led by former vice-president Itamar Franco, had no well-defined economic policy. On the one hand, it maintained the two basic programs launched by Collor (privatization and liberalization), more out of inertia than conviction. On the other hand, it promoted a large fiscal expansion. Federal expenditures jumped 70 percent in real terms over the years 1993–1994, largely due to wage increases for government workers. Fortunately for the administration, tax revenues reached record levels during those two years as the economy recovered, which would obviously keep the public sector's borrowing requirements relatively low (if adjusted for inflation). Also to the Franco administration's credit was its successful conclusion, in April 1994, of an agreement with commercial banks to securitize Brazil's foreign debt under the rules of the so-called Brady Plan.

The economic recovery that began in the last quarter of 1992, after three years of recession, was triggered by the government's fiscal expansion, by the recomposition of the financial wealth of the private sector after Collor's partial confiscation in 1990 (Figure 4.2), by the new inflow of capital to Brazil, and by the growth of the world economy. Despite very high and rising inflation, Brazil's GDP grew 10 percent over the two years 1992–1993.

During that time most analysts of the Brazilian economy agreed that a new stabilization plan would be necessary before the general elections of October 1994, to avoid a reprise of the events of 1989; as the elections approached, political uncertainty would compound the economic uncertainty, and a hyperinflation could result. Franco's administration started working on such a plan only after Senator Fernando Henrique Cardoso became minister of finance in May 1993, bringing with him a team of economists associated with his party, the Brazilian Social Democratic Party (PSDB).

Cardoso's plan, which took shape by the end of 1993 and was officially launched in February 1994, comprised two distinct phases. The first consisted of establishing a new unit of account (the "real unit of value," or URV) equal to U.S.$1, the cruzeiro value of which was adjusted daily according to an average of Brazilian inflation rates. Starting March 1, 1994, prices could be freely denominated in the new unit. At the same time, a new currency was created, the *real*, worth one URV, which would succeed the URV at a future date to be chosen by the administration. Over the following months, prices were voluntarily converted into the new unit, producing an almost complete indexation of the nation's economy to the dollar. By definition, the rate of inflation measured in the URV (the unit of account) is equal to the acceleration of inflation measured in the cruzeiro (the currency unit). Between March and June, when the new unit of account existed, inflation in cruzeiros jumped from 38 percent to 50 percent per month (a cumulative inflation rate of 12 percentage points, measured in URVs).

The synchronization of price adjustments through the URV was designed to minimize relative price movements and to avoid the contamination of the new currency, the *real*, by the old currency, the cruzeiro. On July 1, 1994, the *real* came into existence, and both the cruzeiro and the URV were eliminated.

The choice of the date for implementing the currency reform was clearly motivated by the proximity of the national elections. A sharp drop in the monthly inflation rate from 50 percent per month in June to less than

1 percent in September was the basic reason for the victory of the administration's candidate, Fernando H. Cardoso—"father" of the *Real* Plan—in October. Not only did his party, the PSDB, win the governorships of Brazil's three largest states, but his political coalition, which included the Liberal Front Party (PFL) and smaller parties, won over two-thirds of the seats in the national congress.

In the first six months of the Cardoso plan leading up to the Mexican crisis (July through December 1994), the administration's strategy seemed aimed at rapid monetary stabilization, reaching inflation rates of one digit per year through 1995. To that end the government allowed a nominal appreciation of the exchange rate of about 16 percentage points (from R$1 per U.S.$1 in June to R$0.84 per U.S.$1 in January) and froze public sector prices (for fuels, electric energy, transportation, and telecommunications) for one year. Import tariffs were further reduced in September to increase the supply of consumer goods in the domestic markets. In addition, the central bank imposed high reserve requirements on demand and time deposits in the banking system to reduce the supply of consumer credit and moderate the boom in consumption brought about by the sudden price stability.

At that point there was no concern about the increase in the current-account deficit resulting from the rapid stabilization. After all, the government had started the plan with international reserves of about U.S.$40 billion (equivalent to fifteen months of imports at the time), and the supply of foreign capital to Brazil was elastic. Government officials used to say that the stock of reserves was excessive and a reduction was desirable, and that an increase in the current-account deficit from practically zero to about 2 percent of GDP would be more appropriate to a developing country like Brazil.

It is particularly relevant to examine the exchange rate policy, because it has been the basic instrument used to keep inflation low. Figure 4.3 presents real effective exchange rates since 1989. Contrary to the Brazilian tradition since 1968, when a scheme of minidevaluations was adopted to keep the real exchange rate fairly stable in the face of high and variable inflation, the experience more recently has been much greater variance in exchange rates. Since mid-1992, when capital inflows to Brazil started to assume more consistently large values, the government has allowed a smooth and continual appreciation of the exchange rate. From its peak of mid-1992 to the end of June 1994—that is, before the *real* was introduced—there was a 15 percent real appreciation, which in the second half of 1994 was augmented by an additional 23 percent (representing a compounding of about 35 percent since 1992).

Despite the ongoing appreciation of Brazil's exchange rate, the trade surplus stayed fairly stable at U.S.$12 billion per year (about 2.5 percent of GDP) until the third quarter of 1994. But since the last quarter of the

Figure 4.3   Real Effective Exchange Rate in Brazil (1988 = 100)

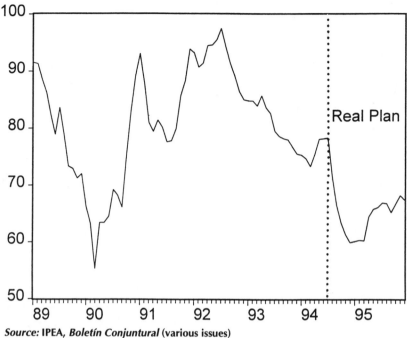

Source: IPEA, *Boletín Conjuntural* (various issues)

year, imports have exploded as a new factor has come into play in addition to the trade liberalization and exchange rate appreciation: a boom in domestic consumer demand (see Figure 4.4).[3]

In the three quarters ending in June 1995, the trade balance turned from a surplus of 2.5 percent of GDP to a deficit of the same magnitude (at an annual rate). As Brazil has a service-account deficit on the order of U.S.$17 billion per year, this means that the current-account deficit went from practically zero until the second quarter of 1994 to $25 billion (about 4 percent of GDP) in the first half of 1995 (at an annual rate).

A significant loss of central bank reserves would not start until December 1994, as capital outflows added to the burgeoning current-account deficit. Foreign exchange reserves peaked at $40.9 billion in September, fell to $36.5 billion in December, and dropped further to $31.7 billion in May 1995.

In the final months of 1994 (before the Mexican crisis), the election results and the initial success of the stabilization plan brought a wave of general optimism in government and business circles, as if structural reform, monetary stability, and economic growth were around the corner.

Figure 4.4   Brazil's Exports, Imports, and Trade Balance, 1990–1995
(annualized and seasonally adjusted in U.S.$ billions)

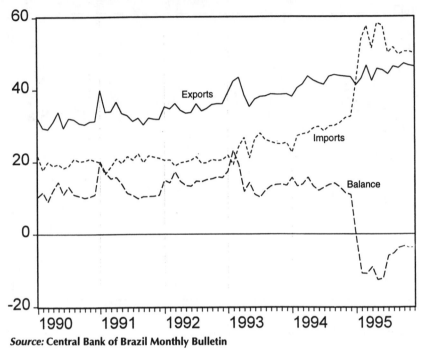

Source: **Central Bank of Brazil Monthly Bulletin**

But the Mexican devaluation on the external front, and the hesitancy of the new Brazilian administration in the first months of 1995, would bring people back to reality.

The Contagion Effect:
Policy Responses in the Cardoso Administration

Cardoso's *Real* Plan created an economic boom in the nine months following its July 1994 introduction, as is usual with stabilization plans that reduce inflation instantaneously. By itself, the transition from 50 percent to 2 percent monthly inflation is estimated to have produced a real income gain of about 12 percent to low- and average-income Brazilians, who represent about 80 percent of the population. Relative price stability and rising employment also encouraged consumers to go into debt. Together, rising incomes and indebtedness stimulated consumption.

The other components of domestic aggregate demand were also on the rise. Federal government expenditures have been expanding at 30 percent annually in real terms since 1993, and it is estimated that gross investment rose from 15 percent of GDP in 1994 to 17 percent in 1995.

Industrial production increased 13.5 percent in the first nine months of the plan relative to the first half of 1994, while GDP expanded 8.7 percent over the same period.

Even without the Mexican collapse, those numbers made it clear that the Brazilian economy was expanding at a rate incompatible with domestic price stability and a sustainable current-account position. The Mexican crisis added two new elements to the scenario. First, it occasioned a small capital flight, as well as a temporary closing of the world capital markets to Brazil, so that all maturities due in the first quarter of 1995 had to be paid. Second, it became obvious that a rapid monetary stabilization strictly based on an exchange rate anchor would now be impossible, since that would require a level of external financing that was now unattainable.

The new Cardoso administration therefore shifted the focus of its economic policy from rapid price stabilization to balance-of-payments equilibrium. The first manifestation of the new priority was a 7 percent real devaluation in the first week of March 1995, with the announcement of an exchange rate band of 0.88/0.93 *reais* per U.S. dollar. At the same time, both to prevent speculative attacks against the *real* and to curb economic activity, the central bank promoted a sharp increase in interest rates, and introduced new credit restrictions.[4]

Starting in March 1995, real borrowing rates by banks were kept at an annualized rate of 25 to 30 percent, and real lending rates as high as a 60 to 70 percent annualized rate—the difference resulting from the high reserve requirements on demand and time deposits, and from the high level of taxation on financial intermediation. Figure 4.5 presents realized real interest rates (deflated by consumer price index [CPI] inflation) and dollar interest rates in Brazil. Since the beginning of 1994, but especially after June of that year, realized dollar interest rates have been incredibly high due to the appreciation of the exchange rate, creating an enormous space for interest arbitrage of short-term funds between the domestic and the foreign financial markets.

The real devaluation and credit squeeze of March produced a sharp economic contraction in the second and third quarters of 1995, bringing with it a reduction of imports and equilibrium in the trade balance. The contraction was accompanied by a liquidity crisis in the private sector spreading to part of the banking system. The central bank's intervention in two large private banks, as well as the bailout of the two largest state-owned banks, threatened a bank panic in the third quarter. A deposit insurance scheme was rapidly implemented, and heavy financial subsidies were extended to private banks to take over the failed banks. By the end of 1995, the liquidity crisis seemed to have been controlled, but not without a significant deterioration in the banks' credit portfolios and still unknown, albeit very large, losses to the federal government in the guise of credit subsidies.

Figure 4.5 Realized *Real* Interest Rates and Dollar Interest Rates in Brazil: 1989–1995 (percent per month)

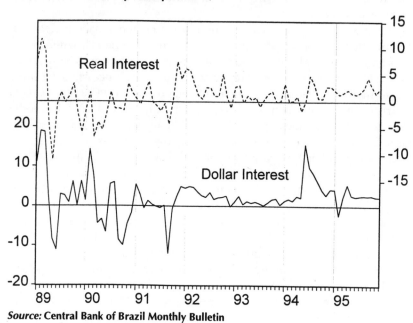

Source: **Central Bank of Brazil Monthly Bulletin**

Also in March, the government introduced restrictions on imports and started by raising tariffs on consumer durables from 20 or 30 percent to 70 percent, aiming especially at automobile imports. A quota system on auto imports announced in June was temporarily suspended due to a trade conflict with Argentina because it violated the agreements of Mercosur. The import restrictions, disguised as "new" industrial policy, represent a retrocession of the trade reform of the past five years. Therefore, one of the pillars of the neoliberal platform (free trade) has been damaged by the change in the international financial conditions brought about by the Mexican crisis.

The gradual dismantling of the credit restrictions and the reduction of real interest rates started in the last quarter of 1995, as the signs of a coming recession and widespread bankruptcies were perceived. As a result, the bottom of the economic contraction was reached in the third quarter, and after that the economy has settled to a low growth path (around 2 to 3 percent per year), a trade balance, and a slightly falling rate of inflation.

The exchange rate band was changed in June 1995 to 0.91/0.99 *reais* to the U.S. dollar, and again in January 1996 to 0.97/1.06. The policy is very similar to the one followed by Mexico until December 1994, although the device used is different. Instead of a preannounced schedule, the device consists of irregular devaluations promoted by the central bank according to the change in the Brazilian wholesale price index (WPI). As wholesale prices tend to increase well below consumer prices under this exchange rate rule, due to the large weight of tradable goods in its composition, the exchange rate serves as a kind of "moving" anchor to domestic prices. The device has been preferred to a fixed exchange rate both because it preserves the discretionary power of the government in adjusting the exchange rate and because it avoids a more intense overvaluation in the initial phase of stabilization. Over time, it is expected that the rate of inflation, measured by consumer prices, will converge to the lower rate of devaluation. In 1995, for instance, CPI inflation was 23 percent, while WPI inflation was only 7 percent. In 1996, it is expected that this gap will be further narrowed. Whether the real exchange rate resulting from this policy will be sustainable in the longer term is an open question. In the case of Mexico, it was not.

A "de-indexation" package was sent to the congress in the last days of June, aiming particularly at the labor market. Since July 1994, the law has guaranteed a minimum annual wage adjustment according to accumulated CPI inflation for private sector workers, allowing free wage negotiation on top of that. The new proposal eliminates this guarantee, although keeping the freedom of the parties to negotiate. The government will set the minimum wage only once a year, stopping its intervention in the labor market.

On the other hand, the Mexican crisis, coming at the moment the new Cardoso administration took office, has not had any effect on the pace and priorities of the economic reforms in Brazil. The agenda is massive: fiscal reform (fiscal federalism and tax, budgetary, and administrative reforms), social security reform, deregulation, privatization, and political reform (of both the party and electoral systems). The Cardoso administration maintained its gradualist reform strategy, based on small and continuous legislative changes, instead of more radical or once-and-for-all changes.

This gradualist approach has been criticized on several grounds. In a country paralyzed by a rigid economic and political structure inherited from decades of interventionism, protectionism, and clientelism, either a radical institutional change occurs in the direction of a new and more efficient economic system, or the old problems (including inflation) recur. Despite the good intentions of the administration and its political and economic competence, small changes are unable to break the old structures and are deemed to fail in the longer term.

President Cardoso missed two opportunities to push for radical reforms: the first was immediately after his election in the first round of the presidential elections in October 1994, still as a senator, and the second soon after the Mexican crisis, when people feared for the future of the *Real* Plan. In both cases, there was support both in public opinion and in the congress for bolder initiatives.

The top priority in the reforming process to sustain the relative monetary stabilization achieved by the *Real* Plan is fiscal reform. Surprisingly, the Cardoso government started proposing changes in the constitutional chapter dealing with the economic order, with two goals: repealing the constitutional discrimination against foreign capital, and moderating the state's rule in the petroleum, gas, and telecommunications monopolies.[5]

The reason for starting here seemed to be the perception by the administration that issues of deregulation would be not only easier for the congress to comprehend but also faster to resolve, as there was more consensus on this topic than others in the fiscal reform agenda. In other words, the executive branch hoped to lead off with a readily achievable success that would pave the way for more difficult issues in the future. In fact, the congress has so far approved, with some modifications, all the executive's proposals concerning the economic order.

Which regulatory models will prevail in reorganizing the electric energy, telecommunications, transportation, gas, and petroleum sectors is not yet clear, since the Cardoso government does not seem to have a well-defined model, and the infraconstitutional legislation has to be approved by the congress. Two predictions are possible to make, however. First, it is very unlikely that the government will completely privatize these key sectors. On the contrary, the administration seems to prefer retaining the state's role in long-range planning of investments, setting priorities, and facilitating joint ventures and concessions to private companies. Second, there is an urgent need for new investments in these industries, which the public sector can ill afford. In short, the regulatory model, whatever its outlines, will have to be attractive to private capital, both domestic and foreign.

Two examples of the timidity of the Cardoso administration are the proposals for changes in the social security system and the so-called administrative reform in the congressional agenda for the first semester of 1996. In both cases, the goal is only to improve the federal budget without attacking the fundamental problems of the federal social security system or public sector organization. Similarly, Cardoso's tax reform proposal represents an attempt to reinforce the federal taxing powers, without making any major change in the distortions and inefficiencies of the Brazilian tax system.

Economic Reform in Brazil:
Lessons from the Recent Past and Challenges Lying Ahead

Any assessment of the current situation in Brazil and the prospects for the future, after two years of the *Real* Plan and eighteen months after the Mexican crisis, has to consider two time lines. In the short run (say, over the next year), it is very likely that inflation will stay at the current level (15 to 20 percent a year), growth will reach a 2 to 3 percent annual rate, and the current-account deficit will stay in the range of 2.5 percent of GDP (implying a trade balance). Given the high liquidity in the world financial markets and the good state of confidence in Brazil, the government can maintain its exchange rate rule, the cornerstone of economic policy.

On the domestic front, it seems that the population and the political system are willing to accept a low rate of growth with rising unemployment and stagnation of real wages based on relative price stability. However, the benefits of low inflation are a once-and-for-all gain, while low growth represents a continuous and cumulative loss over time. One can reasonably assume that at some point political pressures will arise, forcing the government to expand the economy, even at the cost of rising inflation.

Since fiscal policy is very rigid in the short run, and since it has been very expansive in the last three years, the only instrument used to control domestic demand has been monetary and credit policy, leading to very high real interest rates. Although monetary and credit policy can be effective in producing a recession, its fiscal consequences will likely be devastating in Brazil. First, the public sector is the largest debtor in the domestic market, and it is capitalizing a real interest rate of over 20 percent per year on its debt, which is frustrating any effort at fiscal adjustment. Second, low growth impedes the increase in real tax revenues, further complicating the fiscal situation. Third, some sectors of the economy cannot survive long with such high interest rates (agriculture, for example) and therefore will press for credit subsidies, which in turn will further increase government expenditures.

In 1995, the (inflation-adjusted) public sector deficit jumped to 5 percent of GDP, after a small surplus of 1.3 percent in the previous year. The main reason for the fiscal deterioration has been the impact of low inflation on real government expenditures, especially salaries. High inflation was a powerful instrument to reduce real public expenditure through payments arrears to contractors and suppliers, postponement of salary increases, and so forth. A subsidiary but increasingly important cause of fiscal deterioration has been the service of the domestic public debt under the real rates of interest above 20 percent per year.

There is a clear trade-off in Brazil today between inflation and growth. To keep inflation low, the economy cannot grow more than 2 to 3 percent annually, given the balance-of-payments constraints, i.e., the impossibility of running a current-account deficit of more than 2 to 2.5 percent of GDP. Deficits higher than that increase the country's dependency on short-term capital flows, risking speculative crises like the one that hit Mexico in December 1994 and Argentina soon after. Inflation is kept low by a continuous overvaluation of the exchange rate coupled with very high real interest rates. The high cost of capital in the country inhibits investment, while the overvalued exchange rate leads to the stagnation of exports. In this way, the two basic factors for sustainable growth in any economy are being lost.

Three mutually reinforcing alternatives to get rid of this trade-off can be identified: fiscal reform, privatization/deregulation, and higher competitiveness. A profound fiscal reform that balanced the public sector budgets on a reliable basis would allow the substitution of the exchange rate anchor by a monetary-fiscal anchor with two positive consequences. First, it would give the central bank effective conditions to control the monetary aggregates and to stabilize the ratio of the domestic public debt to GDP, with the goal of keeping inflation low and stable. Second, it would allow a substantial reduction of real interest rates, stimulating investment, improving public finances, and reducing the inflow of speculative capital. A reduction of the capital inflow would naturally lead to a real depreciation of the currency, stimulating exports and allowing imports to grow.

The second alternative is to accelerate the privatization program (especially in the key sectors of energy, petroleum and gas, telecommunications, and transportation) and the deregulation of the economy (especially the labor and financial markets, and protected sectors like ports). This would at the same time stimulate foreign direct investment and improve the competitiveness of Brazilian products.

The third alternative is to reduce the so-called "Brazil cost" or the higher cost of domestic production vis-à-vis other competing countries. Here the critical factors are tax reform, in the sense of reducing the tax burden on domestic production; the reduction in the cost of capital (both of real interest rates and the domestic price of capital goods); the deregulation of protected sectors; and substantial improvements in economic and social infrastructure.

Although the Cardoso administration has stressed the need to make progress in all these directions, the fact is that after eighteen months in office its proposals and actions have been timid, slow, and compromising. In the face of his first eighteen months in government, it seems that President Cardoso has two courses of action. The first is to accelerate the structural reforms to gradually overcome the current inflation growth trade-off by abandoning the exchange rate anchor, fostering growth in 1997–1998, and paving the way for his reelection in 1998. The second is to maintain his compromising policy, which is incapable of changing the institutions and structures within which the government operates. In this case, the scenario will be one of low inflation and near stagnation in the next three years, with increasing risk of some sort of economic crisis. Like Mexico, Brazil is starting to face the difficulty of abandoning the temporary anchor (the exchange rate) that produced the spectacular, albeit temporary, fall of inflation. Without radical structural changes, which the administration does not seem willing to fight for, it is likely that Brazil will follow a path similar to that of Mexico.

Finally, it has also been argued that the vices of the Brazilian electoral and party systems will make it almost impossible to produce the profound reforms in the structure of government that the country so urgently needs for its continuing economic and social development. The fragmented political system has made it impossible to form stable majorities in the national congress, and therefore impossible for the executive to follow time-consistent policies. It also implies the capacity of minority interests to block any major change to the benefit of the society at large. A courageous change in the electoral and party systems, in the direction of attributing more responsibility to the political class for government policies and for the economic and social demands of the population, must be made to improve governability and install a working democracy in the country.

Conclusions

Brazil has lagged behind other major Latin American countries in achieving relative monetary stability and in modernizing its economic and political institutions. The country started to move on those agendas five years ago with Collor's election, but it was unable to follow a consistent path toward modernization because a political crisis cut short the president's mandate in late 1992. After the interim Franco administration, the elections of October 1994 installed Cardoso with basically the same economic platform, in the wake of a stabilization program that reduced inflation overnight from 50 to 2 percent per month.

The challenges of the new Cardoso government are to maintain the relative monetary stability achieved in 1995 by correcting its short-run economic policy, while promoting the needed institutional and economic reforms that will create a favorable environment for long-term stability and growth.

The Mexican devaluation of December 1994, which caused an immediate contraction in international capital markets, came at the moment Cardoso took office and led to a shift in the government's priority from rapid monetary stabilization to balance-of-payments equilibrium. That shift in emphasis has three important implications. First, monetary stabilization, in the sense of one-digit inflation rates, is likely out of reach in the short run. Second, growth will have to be modest (no more than 2 to 3 percent annually) to avoid domestic inflationary pressures and maintain equilibrium in the trade balance. Third, a retrogression in the opening of the Brazilian trade system is in progress, disguised as a new industrial policy, as an auxiliary instrument to keep the current-account deficit at a maximum level of 2.5 percent of GDP. Despite a comfortable level of international reserves, Brazil has been increasingly vulnerable to short-term capital movements, and the only way to reduce vulnerability is by keeping a sustainable current-account position.

A courageous move from a loose to a tight fiscal policy in the short run would allow the central bank to alleviate the credit restrictions distorting financial intermediation and reduce the still incredibly high real interest rates needed to support the overvalued exchange rate. Then a more realistic exchange rate policy, probably implying a real devaluation, could be adopted, avoiding a larger than necessary recession to produce a balance-of-payments equilibrium. However, given the institutional rigidities and the timidity of the administration, the space for fiscal tightening is not large. This means that the conditions for lifting the exchange rate anchor, the cornerstone of the government's economic policy, will probably not be present in the near future.

In the medium term, after its initial success in passing the constitutional changes on the economic order in congress, the Cardoso administration must define a strategy to attack the more difficult items on the agenda, starting with fiscal reform covering the tax system, fiscal federalism, social security, and administration. So far, the government's proposals in all these areas have been timid and compromising and have avoided the fundamental issues involved. It is achievements in fiscal reform that will largely determine the path of monetary stabilization and growth in Brazil over the coming years. But unless President Cardoso's piecemeal strategy of reform is modified, there is little hope for true fiscal reform in Brazil.

Finally, regarding monetary stabilization per se, it seems that Mexico's (and to a lesser extent Argentina's) long experience with the exchange rate–based stabilization model has not been fully grasped in Brazil, especially the longer-term conditions for shifting nominal anchors. In Mexico, the adjustment of relative prices between nontradable and tradable goods to a sustainable long-run equilibrium came suddenly through a foreign exchange rate crisis that produced a large devaluation and a deep recession. In Argentina, given the legal fixation of the exchange rate, the relative price adjustment is occurring through a deflation of nontradable goods prices (including nominal wages) brought about by a prolonged economic recession with unemployment rates close to 20 percent of the labor force. It is not yet clear which of these paths Brazil will follow, or whether it will be feasible to shift anchors smoothly (say, from the exchange rate to a monetary aggregate, under the support of a sound fiscal policy), thus avoiding the high economic costs incurred by both Mexico and Argentina since 1995. In any case, it is clear that Brazil will face a "stabilization crisis" of some kind in the near future.

Notes

1. Inflation in Brazil was 1,600 percent in 1990 and 1,200 percent in 1994. The data reported in the text are from the Economic Commission for Latin America, *Balance Preliminar de la Economía de América Latina y el Caribe* (Santiago, Chile: ECLAC, various issues).

2. The index is computed by IPEA, *Boletim Conjuntural,* Rio de Janeiro (various issues).

3. Figure 4.4 presents seasonally adjusted monthly data for exports and imports at an annual rate, according to Central Bank of Brazil statistics.

4. In May 1995, the rural representation in the congress obtained from the executive an annual interest rate of 16 percent on rural credit and the restructuring of rural debts for seven years, while the cost of funds to the government is in the range of 32 percent per year and the maturity of the federal debt is about two months. At the same time, most Brazilian states face a deep financial crisis as the result of past expenditure increases financed by "snowball" indebtedness. The federal government is refinancing long term a large part of state debts and advancing some fresh money to states as a means of avoiding a complete breakdown of state administrations.

5. The constitution of 1988 distinguished between Brazilian-owned and foreign-owned enterprises, serving to support a host of administrative discriminations against foreign capital imposed by the government bureaucracy with or without legal support. Moreover, there were restrictions in the participation of foreign capital in areas such as mining, coastal navigation, and electric energy. All these restrictions were removed in 1995.

5

The Mexican Peso Crisis and Argentina's Convertibility Plan: Monetary Virtue or Monetary Impotence?

Roberto Bouzas[1]

The Convertibility Plan has been a cornerstone of President Carlos Saúl Menem's economic policies. Launched in March 1991, its main features were to make the Argentine currency convertible into U.S. dollars at a fixed nominal exchange rate and to back the monetary base fully with the central bank's international reserves. In the four subsequent years, the Convertibility Plan led Argentina to an unprecedented period of falling inflation rates and rapid economic growth.

This performance was facilitated by the favorable international financial environment of the years 1991–1993. The rise of U.S. interest rates after February 1994 and the plummeting of the Mexican peso in December 1994 brought the Argentine expansion to a halt. By early 1995, the economy was sliding into recession, while capital flight and a run on bank deposits seemed the prelude to a crippling financial crisis. The effects of the Mexican crisis were further compounded by the political uncertainties posed by the forthcoming presidential elections.

To address the critical situation, the Menem government stuck to the currency board mechanism and implemented a very restrictive fiscal program with the financial support of the International Monetary Fund (IMF) and the multilateral banks. In the short term, the government's response proved effective in preventing the worst-case scenario: unabated capital flight and financial collapse. Furthermore, the swift response was instrumental in the government's electoral success in the elections of May 1995.

By mid-year, as bank deposits started to recover, the worst seemed to have been left behind. Yet improved conditions in financial markets were not paralleled by economic recovery. During 1995, the economy remained in a depressed state, which continued into 1996. Emerging from the recession has thus become a key issue for policymakers in Buenos Aires.

Some observers have interpreted the short-term success of the Convertibility Plan and its survival (as opposed to the pervasive disruption of the economy and of policymaking in Mexico) as a vindication of rules compliance and "monetary virtue." Others, though, point to Argentina as a case in which maintaining an archaic policy regime has taken precedence over adjusting to changes in the external environment.[2] Both arguments may be mistakenly posing the issue, however. Far from being a controlled experiment of the virtues and shortcomings of fixed versus flexible exchange rates, the distinct policy responses of the Mexican and Argentine governments during 1994–1995 underscore fundamental differences between the two countries' economic institutions and recent economic performances.

This chapter traces the broad outlines of Argentina's economic record in the 1990s and the early repercussions of the 1994 Mexican crisis for policymaking and the economy. The first section outlines the strengths and weaknesses of the Convertibility Plan prior to the Mexican devaluation. The second section deals with the government's handling of fallout from the Mexican crisis in the first half of 1995, underlining the twin objectives of preventing financial collapse and avoiding a public sector default. The third section reviews the response of the government and the economy after the initial phase of crisis management, in particular with regard to the performance of the financial and the external sectors and the role played by private markets and public institutions in the process. The fourth section deals with the medium-term prospects for the Argentine economy, emphasizing the dilemmas posed by the need to restore economic growth and reduce external fragility. The chapter ends with a brief overview of Argentina's economic challenges and alternatives given the country's recent policy record and the general international financial environment.

The Convertibility Plan Before the Mexican Crisis

To be understood properly, the economic reform and stabilization program of the first Menem administration (1989–1995) must be placed within the broader context of the economic performance during the preceding decade, severely constrained by the external and domestic transfer problems caused by the debt crisis.

Argentina's external transfer problem revolved around the need to generate enough foreign exchange to service the nation's external debt. The domestic transfer problem, in turn, derived from the fiscal repercussions of the external debt crisis. The ensuing vicious circle of large devaluations, fiscal collapse, and high inflation culminated in hyperinflation in 1989 and 1990. In the process, not only did economic growth, financial intermediation, and public finances suffer, but the state itself as an economic agent and political institution came to the verge of collapse.[3]

Following the demise of the Radical Civic Union (UCR) government in mid-1989, the Menem administration initiated a structural reform program consisting of aggressive privatization, deregulation, and foreign trade and financial liberalization. The privatization program served two purposes: it removed a financial burden and it provided the public sector with fresh cash and debt reduction. It was also hoped that, in the medium term, privatization would help improve economic efficiency. Within a relatively short time, the government privatized most public utilities (electricity generation, transmission, and distribution; telecommunications; domestic and international airlines; gas pipelines and local distribution networks; water and sewage systems; cargo and passenger railways; and highway maintenance works, among others); it also sold off most of its interests in goods-producing sectors such as coal, steel, and oil and natural gas.[4]

Deregulation also proceeded rapidly—in goods, services, and, to a lesser extent, labor markets. A prominent example was in the oil and gas industries. Traditionally under the control of public monopolies and stringent government regulations, oil and natural gas production and distribution were transferred to private capital and subjected to open competition. Financial and commodity markets (such as those for cereals, tobacco, sugar, and meat) also experienced far-reaching deregulation. Labor markets underwent a similar process, albeit at a slower pace.

Similarly overhauled were Argentina's foreign trade and payments regimes. Nominal import protection fell significantly, while the tariff structure was simplified. By 1991, all export taxes and most quantitative restrictions (except for the automobile sector) had been phased out. Liberalization of the foreign exchange market and the capital account was even more radical. In late 1989, the government removed all restrictions on foreign exchange transactions and all barriers to foreign investment, both direct and portfolio, making Argentina's capital market one of the most open in the world.

Parallel to these structural reforms, during 1989 and 1990 the Menem administration made a number of failed attempts to bring inflation under control. Only after the launching of the Convertibility Plan in April 1991 did the administration succeed in sharply reducing the inflation rate. As noted at the outset, the plan pegged the Argentine peso to the U.S. dollar at a fixed nominal exchange rate and fully backed the monetary base with the central bank's international reserves. The central bank was thus legally prohibited from financing budget deficits through the printing press, turning fiscal adjustment into an overriding priority.

The most remarkable achievement of the Convertibility Plan was the subsequent combination of a rapid jump in output and investment, and falling inflation rates. As shown in Table 5.1, between 1990 and 1994, real gross domestic product (GDP) expanded by an accumulated 34.8 percent, led by rising gross domestic investment (which expanded 121.6 percent from the depressed levels of 1990). By 1994, the investment-to-GDP rate had reached 20 percent, the highest level since the mid-1980s. Consumer spending also experienced rapid growth in the initial years of the plan, but after 1993 its rate of expansion fell behind that of the GDP. Although domestic savings recovered as a result, by 1994 the savings rate was still below the levels of the 1980s. The investment-savings gap was financed by a generous inflow of foreign capital stimulated by the favorable international economic environment. Inflation, in turn, tumbled from a 4,900 percent annual rate in 1989 to just over 3 percent in 1994.

Nevertheless, prosperity under the Convertibility Plan was not shared equally. The most disturbing development was a steady increase in unemployment. Although an estimated 300,000 new jobs were created between May 1991 and October 1994, the unemployment rate doubled to reach an unprecedented 12.2 percent by the latter date. Initially, along with rising unemployment came rising labor force participation rates, as more Argentines looked for jobs. But since October 1993, there has been a net reduction in total employment. Key determinants here were the far-reaching process of public sector divestitures (which trimmed jobs in many service

Table 5.1   The Convertibility Plan in the "Boom" Years: Indicators of Economic Performance, 1990–1994

	1990	1991	1992	1993	1994
Good news					
1. Real GDP (annual rate of growth, %)[a]	0.1	8.9	8.7	6.0	0.074
2. Consumer prices (annual rate of growth, end of period, %)	1,344.0	0.841	17.5	7.4	3.9
3. Investment rates (% of GDP)[b]	14.0	14.6	16.7	18.4	20.0
4. Public sector balance (% of GDP)[c]	−3.1	−2.5	−0.1	0.8	−0.4
Bad news					
1. Trade balance (in millions U.S.$)	8,276	3,702	−2,637	−3,668	−5,752
2. Current account balance (in millions U.S.$)	4,832	−259	−6,440	−7,804	−10,243
3. Real exchange rate (index, 1986=100)[d]	92.1	80.7	79.8	80.4	80.0
4. Unemployment rate (%)[e]	6.3	6.0	7.0	9.3	12.2
5. Real wages (index, 1991=100)	112.6	100.0	95.0	93.5	94.2

Sources: Ministry of the Economy, *Informe económico* (Buenos Aires: various issues); Institute of Statistics and Censuses, *Encuesta permanente de hogares* (Buenos Aires: various issues); Center of International Economics, *Comercio exterior argentino* (Buenos Aires, various issues); Foundation for Latin American Economic Research, *Indicadores de coyuntura* (Buenos Aires, various issues).

[a]Based on 1986 constant prices.

[b]Based on gross fixed investments at current prices.

[c]Based on the global surplus/deficit of the national public sector, excluding privatization proceeds.

[d]Deflated by the wholesale price index.

[e]Based on October data for each year. Employment surveys are conducted in May and October.

industries) and firm restructuring and plant closings in the private sector. Rising unemployment was of particular concern because Argentina lacks a safety net for those temporarily or permanently falling behind in the economy.

Aside from these equity issues, even before the Mexican crisis the Convertibility Plan experienced problems in three interconnected areas: relative prices, the budget balance, and the external sector. Before discussing the impact of the devaluation of the Mexican peso, it is important to examine each of these in turn.

Relative Prices

The Convertibility Plan was born with an exchange rate problem inherited from the floating exchange rate experience of 1990. Aggravating that problem in the early years of the plan were the rapid growth of domestic demand and the imperfect arbitrage of goods markets, which postponed convergence between domestic and international inflation rates. This misalignment was compounded by the fact that the fixed nominal exchange rate was the anchor of the government's stabilization plan and of its credibility within and outside the country.

Initially, the government expected that the downward adjustment of prices and wages and faster productivity growth (fueled by deregulation of domestic markets and foreign competition) would raise the real exchange rate.[5] When that failed to take place to the extent required, policymakers implemented a number of direct fiscal measures geared to reduce domestic costs and improve the relative prices of tradables. These included the reduction or selective elimination of distortive taxes (such as local indirect taxes and payroll taxes) and the provision of direct incentives to the tradable goods-producing sectors (such as tax rebates for exports). But these actions entailed a fiscal cost, which posed an additional policy dilemma.

Between March 1991 and December 1994, the consumer price index (CPI) increased by an accumulated 58.8 percent. The wholesale price index (WPI), in turn, rose by 12.4 percent. However, the performance of relative prices began to change after 1994.[6] Yet, added to the sharp increase in productivity and changes in the tax structure, this was not enough to compensate completely for the misalignment. Overall, the structure of relative prices favored the allocation of resources toward the production of nontradables.

The Fiscal Stance

The fiscal adjustment achieved in the 1991–1994 period was remarkable, as shown by the drop in public sector deficits (see Table 5.1). Yet at the root of the adjustment were an increase in tax receipts (facilitated by a simplification of the tax code and high levels of economic activity) and large-scale privatization.[7] Furthermore, the trade-off between the need to reduce the domestic cost of tradables and to maintain fiscal discipline intensified as economic growth became more heavily dependent on net exports and investment spending after 1994. These constraints were aggravated by the difficulty federal authorities had in controlling spending by provincial governments and by the overhaul of the social security (retirement) system. The political cycle also played a role in 1994.[8]

The worsening fiscal stance was obvious but still far from dramatic before the devaluation of the Mexican peso in December 1994, as revealed by the small public sector deficit recorded in that year.[9] However, unable to meet the stringent fiscal targets negotiated with the IMF and reluctant to backslide from its "supply-side" policies, in September 1994 the Argentine government, as anticipated, concluded the three-year Extended Fund Facility (EFF) agreement it had signed with the IMF in 1992.[10]

Pressures to improve fiscal performance were hence clear even before the Mexican crisis. In November 1994, the government canceled all undisbursed spending for the remainder of the year (except for salaries) and decided on a U.S.$1 billion reduction in authorized spending for the 1995 budget. Consistency between the rigid monetary scheme and fiscal policy had become critical, as conditions in international financial markets worsened after early 1994.

The External Sector

The Convertibility Plan was also accompanied by a steady deterioration of Argentina's trade and current-account balances. After reaching a peak surplus of U.S.$8.3 billion in 1990, the trade balance plunged to an unprecedented $5.8 billion deficit in 1994. The main contributing factor was the rapid growth of imports, which increased fivefold from the depressed levels of 1990. Exports, in turn, expanded by slightly over a fourth, to reach $15.7 billion in 1994. The current-account deficit increased tenfold over the same period, to $10 billion in 1994.

The rise in imports and the trade deficit were the outgrowths of trade liberalization, real appreciation of the domestic currency, and rapid growth of domestic demand. But it was abundant external finance that paved the road to the imbalance. In fact, foreign capital inflows were sufficient to account not only for the current-account deficit but to increase the central bank's international reserves from $4.8 billion in 1989 to over $16 billion in 1994.

After February 1994, however, rising U.S. interest rates gradually dried up external financial sources and increased the cost of borrowing. In 1994, net private capital inflows fell by 36 percent, to $8.9 billion for the year as a whole, from the record-breaking level of $14 billion in the previous year. In the context of larger current-account deficits and shrinking capital inflows, international reserve assets increased by a slight $500 million in 1994, as compared to an average annual increase of $3.7 billion over the preceding four years. Although the government was still floating debt as late as November 1994, the international financial environment had clearly changed.

Large capital inflows during the early 1990s were reminiscent of the period preceding the 1982 debt crisis, which had its own rapid growth in domestic demand, large trade deficits, and real appreciation of the domestic currency. Yet several distinctions were also evident: the relatively more solid fiscal stance of the government and the fact that most of the new investment was private, presumably leading to a more efficient allocation of resources. As the Mexican crisis would demonstrate, however, mounting trade and current-account deficits were unsustainable in the medium term.

The Mexican Devaluation and Crisis Management in Argentina

During the period 1991–1994, Argentina and Mexico shared a number of experiences as regards economic performance. On the one hand, economic growth was facilitated by easy access to international capital markets and was driven by sizable foreign capital inflows. On the other hand, domestic currencies experienced a real appreciation in both countries as the nominal exchange rate was geared toward keeping the inflation rate under control.

But there were also differences—for example, the extent of each economy's dependence on foreign capital inflows. Whereas in Mexico the increase in external savings (as a share of GDP) between 1991 and 1994 provided more resources than needed to finance the increase in gross domestic investment (the excess was the counterpart of a contraction in the domestic savings rate), in Argentina the increase in the external savings rate financed only 59 percent of the total increase in the investment rate.[11]

Despite this and other differences (as explained below), the Mexican crisis of December 20, 1994, affected Argentina very severely (see Table 5.2). In effect, after the devaluation of the Mexican peso, Argentine policies were focused on crisis management. The government moved quickly to secure emergency external support, eliminate the public sector borrowing requirement (indeed attempting to produce a fiscal overkill), and prevent a full-blown financial crisis. Reversing negative market expectations played a critical role in the response.

As noted earlier, the problems the Convertibility Plan faced were not entirely new. A fiscal deficit had reappeared in the second half of 1994, and the supply of external capital had been shrinking since early 1994. It was also well known that the authorities had limited instruments available to intervene in monetary and financial markets.

Table 5.2   The Convertibility Plan in 1995: Adjustment to the Mexican Crisis

	1991–94 (Annual Average)	1995
1. Real GDP (rate of growth, %)[a]	7.3	–3.5[b]
2. Unemployment rate (%)[c]	8.6	16.4
3. Stock of deposits in the banking system (rate of growth, %)[d]	45.4	–1.4
4. Value of exports, fob (rate of growth, %)	9.8	31.9
5. Value of imports, cif (rate of growth, %)	37.7	–7.5
6. Trade balance (annual average, millions U.S.$)	–2,089	929
7. Current account deficit (% of GDP)	24	1.1
8. Net capital inflows (millions U.S.$)	8,675	1,500
9. Change in international reserves (millions U.S.$)[e]	2,019	–3,790

Sources: Ministry of the Economy, *Informe económico* (Buenos Aires, various issues); Institute of Statistics and Censuses, *Encuesta permanente de hogares* (Buenos Aires, various issues); Center of International Economics, *Comercio exterior argentino* (Buenos Aires, various issues); Foundation for Latin American Economic Research, *Indicadores de coyuntura* (Buenos Aires, various issues).
[a]Based on 1986 constant prices.
[b]Estimated.
[c]Based on October data.
[d]Total peso and U.S. dollar–denominated deposits at year-end.
[e]At year-end.

The Mexican crisis not only halted foreign capital inflows into Argentina but indeed reversed them. This led to a sharp contraction in international reserves and banking deposits. In the five-month period between December 1994 and the May 1995 presidential elections, total bank deposits in Argentina fell by U.S.$8 billion—tantamount to 17.6 percent of total deposits at the start of the period (see Figure 5.1). The central bank's international reserves, in turn, fell by almost a third, from $16 billion in December 1994 to $11.2 billion in mid-May.[12] As suggested by rising interest rates and the sharp increase in the country-risk premium, Argentina was experiencing a typical run against the domestic currency (and the banking system).

Official statements that tried to minimize the severity of the problems and to present Argentina's case as different from that of Mexico were of dubious effectiveness. Thus, the early attempt of the government to buy time and reach the May presidential elections without paying the full costs of an adjustment package soon proved unfeasible. Uncertainty and pessimism were rife, particularly on the part of foreign investors.

Unfolding events led the government to rapidly abandon this soft approach. By late February 1995, the economic situation had turned so fragile that inaction threatened immediate financial collapse. Thus, in the first four months of 1995, the Menem administration implemented progressively tougher policies in both the fiscal and financial realms, hoping to

Figure 5.1   Bank Deposits and the "Tequila Effect"

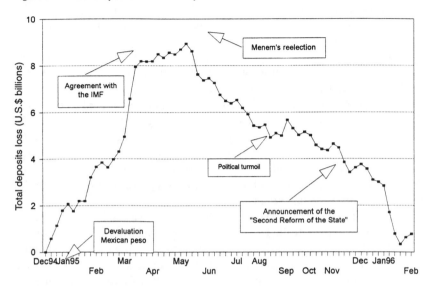

persuade economic agents that the government was resolved to support the economic program whatever the short-term political considerations.[13]

Averting Financial Collapse

The run against the domestic currency and financial system presented the government with an extraordinary challenge. Even before the Mexican crisis, the authorities were fully aware of the weaknesses of the Argentine financial system and had taken measures to strengthen its foundations. Their approach was a long-term one: raise capital-adequacy ratios, provide guidelines for portfolio assessment, and stimulate mergers and acquisitions. The deteriorating economic environment posed a clear-cut dilemma, however, between the long-term interests of survival of the fittest and the short-term need to stave off a financial blow.

The first explicit move to cope with negative expectations was made in mid-January, when monetary authorities went a step further toward full "dollarization" of the economy. By one stroke of the pen the central bank reduced the banking industry's foreign exchange risk by converting U.S.$3.1 billion of banking reserves on peso-denominated deposits into dollars. As a result, one-third of the nation's monetary base was automatically "dollarized." The authorities expected that this decision would clearly signal the government's resolve to hold to the Convertibility Plan and the fixed nominal exchange rate. Simultaneously, but constrained by the limited instruments at their disposal, the authorities provided the banks

with rediscounts and entered into repurchase agreements to provide liquidity in modest amounts.[14] Monetary authorities also organized a "voluntary safety net" to prevent bank closures. But this timid strategy soon
proved unworkable.

The magnitude of the deposits withdrawn, the clash of interest among
private banks, and growing uncertainty as to the short-term prospects for
the economy demanded a more decisive involvement of the authorities in
the management of the crisis. The government therefore issued a decree reforming the central bank's charter and authorizing monetary authorities to
use "excess reserves" to assist those institutions experiencing liquidity
problems.[15] Selected institutions continued to be favored with discretionary relaxation of technical coefficients or carry-forwards. There is no
doubt that this emergency support limited the contraction of total credit
that might otherwise have taken place.

By the end of the first quarter of 1995, the troubles of the financial system were far from controlled. An accelerated rate of withdrawn deposits in
the first half of April led the economic authorities to implement a compulsory deposit insurance scheme aimed at reducing depositors' uncertainty.
They also announced the establishment of two trust funds to foster the reform of the private and provincial banking systems by allowing capitaliza-
tion of troubled institutions and by stimulating mergers and acquisitions.[16]

The trust funds, particularly the private sector one, were not used extensively. Many troubled institutions refrained from asking for support because—with the tolerance of monetary authorities—they transferred part
of the burden of adjustment to their depositors through compulsory
reschedulings. In turn, the May elections and the clear-cut victory of President Menem (who won with 50 percent of the vote) reversed the deposit
drainage. As deposits began to recover, the risk of a traumatic process of
bank restructuring receded. It is remarkable that when deposits started to
recover after the elections, only two institutions were liquidated and five
suspended, all of them small banks.

Back to the IMF

The evolution of relations with multilateral institutions (particularly the
IMF) is also indicative of the policymakers' evolving assessments of the
magnitude of the crisis and the need to take decisive action. In early January, the official stance still was that Argentina did not need IMF support
and that there were "fundamental" differences with IMF officials over the
most appropriate policy approach, particularly with respect to tax policy.
Yet the government's strategy of financing its borrowing requirements in
domestic capital markets soon became untenable.

In February, the authorities announced that Argentina would submit to
IMF monitoring through a mechanism of "enhanced supervision," but that

no request for new loans was envisaged. Within a few weeks, however, they announced a one-year extension of the 1992 EFF agreement and launched a new and comprehensive fiscal and financial package. The government also obtained fresh funds from the World Bank, the Inter-American Development Bank, and the Japanese Export-Import Bank. A specially tailored "Argentine bond" was also part of the deal.[17]

In addition to its rapprochement with the IMF, the government shifted its fiscal priorities. Although there had been two previous adjustments to the 1995 budget (in late 1994 and February 1995), the package announced in March was qualitatively different.[18] Whereas the earlier ones revolved around spending cuts (including public sector salaries) and a widening of the tax base, the March adjustment included a significant tax hike, the major issue in dispute with the IMF.[19] If anything, the new package looked like a temporary resignation of "supply-side" policies geared to improving competitiveness in the wake of the fixed nominal exchange rate.

The new package was expected to yield a total public sector surplus of U.S.$4.4 billion, including $2.4 billion in proceeds from privatization. The result would zero out the government's borrowing requirement for 1995, generating sufficient resources to cancel not only the interest on the public debt but also all the principal due in 1995. In addition to this strategy of fiscal overkill, the administration intensified its pressure on the congress to pass new economic reform laws.[20]

Beyond Crisis Management

At first glance, the timing of the Mexican crisis could not have been more inconvenient for the reelection of President Menem. The economic turbulence that followed took place in the middle of the presidential campaign. Yet the tough fiscal program launched in March, the persistent turbulence in financial markets, and the uncertain economic environment did not prevent Carlos Menem from obtaining a decisive electoral victory in May. In contrast to what happened in 1989, when President Alfonsín transferred the office to Menem six months in advance of schedule, this time the incumbent was able to prevent a collapse of the economy and win the elections by a comfortable margin.[21]

The contrasts between the earlier and lastest episodes are threefold. As far as the economic environment is concerned, in 1989 Argentina's public sector accounts were in complete disarray, the external debt had accumulated into massive arrears, and international reserves were almost exhausted. In 1994, by contrast, the public sector deficit was slim, the country had been enjoying continuous access to voluntary external lending since 1991, and international reserves were comparatively high. The second difference is that, unlike in 1989, the central feature of the 1991 stabilization program was largely unchallenged. In fact, albeit grudgingly, the largest opposition parties had taken the fixed nominal exchange rate and full convertibility as given constraints.[22] Finally, in 1995, the business and financial elites, both domestic and foreign, were strongly behind official policies, as demonstrated by the rapid renegotiation of the suspended EFF agreement with the IMF and the successful subscription of the U.S.$2 billion "Argentine bond."

Two other underlying factors played a role in the president's ability to sustain a majority coalition in favor of official policies amidst such widespread economic uncertainty and hardship. First was the public's relatively fresh memory of hyperinflation and general economic disruption at the turn of the decade. The second was that, at least in the eyes of the electorate, the Menem administration seemed more able than any of its contenders to deal with the still unfolding economic problems. With the Radicals divided and the center-left coalition (Frepaso) still untested, the opposition did not offer credible alternatives.

Menem's convincing reelection was viewed in Argentina and elsewhere as an indicator of the legitimacy and political clout his administration would enjoy in its second term. That impression did not last long, however. When the May unemployment rate, a whopping 18.4 percent, was announced in July, the government suffered a strong blow: the recession looked as if it would be deeper and more prolonged than initially expected.

After the May elections, the government enjoyed some positive economic news, however. First, as political uncertainty subsided, deposits in the banking system started to recover rapidly, easing the strains in the financial system. Second, external financial needs contracted under the influence of a rapid shift to a surplus trade balance. Both developments took place in the context of a forthcoming international financial environment (falling interest rates and a bull market) and continuing support from the IMF.

Deposits Return to the Banks

Immediately after the elections, peso- and dollar-denominated deposits began to recover rapidly (see Figure 5.1). Although their rate of growth slowed down beginning in August, they rebounded by November to reach precrisis levels by February 1996. Several factors help explain this performance, including: the political environment and its effect on expectations, the manner in which the financial restructuring process occurred, and more effective official policies.

The decisive influence of expectations and the political environment was clear-cut. In effect, in the period immediately after the elections (between mid-May and late June), slightly over 40 percent of total deposits withdrawn during the height of the crisis returned to the banks. In contrast, during August and September, the rate of deposit growth was brought almost to a halt as a result of the government's internal strifes. Once these were ironed out in November, deposits began to recover rapidly again to reach precrisis levels by late February 1996. Confirmation of the economics minister and announcement of the so-called second reform of the state by year-end significantly improved market expectations, leading to a rapid recovery of deposits even in the peso-denominated segment of the market (suggesting a fall in exchange rate risk).

The fact that the financial system was able to avoid a traumatic shake-up was another positive factor. In effect, the initial fears that there would be a large number of bank closures and a collapse of the payments chain did not materialize. Indeed, the financial sector went through (and is still undergoing) a major transformation, but not as the result of a financial crash. By year-end the number of financial institutions had dropped by almost a fourth, but only a handful had been closed and liquidated by the authorities. Most of this concentration took place through mergers and acquisitions and went largely unnoticed by the general public. This drop in the number of financial institutions was also accompanied by an increase in the share of the largest—and relatively more solid—banks in total deposits, and by a higher degree of "dollarization" in both assets and liabilities.[23]

The contribution of regulatory policies was slightly different from that originally envisaged. In effect, the trust fund created to advance the restructuring of the private banking system remained largely unused. By contrast, monetary authorities increased their efforts to strengthen the banking system. In a reform announced in August 1995, they replaced the old non–interest bearing reserve requirements system with a new one based on liquidity requirements. The new system was expected to improve liquidity, providing a more efficient "shock absorber," and to reduce the "tax burden" on banks. These decisions, together with high allowances for unrecoverable loans, high minimum capital requirements, and rapid information flow for rating debtors in force since 1994, hopefully helped reduce systemic risk.

Two factors helped prevent the worst-case scenario: the financial sector avoided a crash and deposits recovered. But credit to the private sector remained stagnant or expanded very slowly. Initially, financial institutions were reluctant to lend and preferred to improve their own liquidity ratios instead. But even when interest rates began to fall later in the year, consumers and firms refrained from incurring new debt. This was the result of uncertainty regarding the future course of the economy, low real incomes, already high levels of indebtedness (by historical standards), and an exhaustion of pent-up demand for consumer durables during the 1991–1994 boom.

The External Sector Adjusts

Argentina's trade and current-account balances experienced a remarkable adjustment immediately after the Mexican crisis. Figures for the first three quarters of 1995 indicate that the current account deficit fell from U.S.$7 billion to $1 billion as compared to the previous year. This performance was largely the result of a significant turnaround in the trade balance, which shifted from a record $5.8 billion deficit in 1994 to a $929 million surplus in 1995.

Most remarkably, the turnaround in the trade balance was the result of rapid export growth and moderate import contraction. In effect, during 1995 exports expanded by 31.9 percent, whereas imports contracted by 7.5 percent. The reason behind import contraction was straightforward: the fall in aggregate demand. In turn, rapid export growth was aided by the slack in domestic demand, high international commodity prices, the demand "boom" in Brazil, and productivity gains.

This sizable adjustment accommodated the sharp contraction of foreign capital inflows that followed the Mexican crisis. In effect, for the January–September period, Argentina recorded a U.S.$2.3 billion total capital outflow (concentrated in the first quarter of the year), as compared to a total inflow of $6.3 billion during the same period in 1994. This turnaround was basically a result of the behavior of the private sector, which responded swiftly to events in Mexico (particularly in the January–March period). Had there not been substantial inflow of foreign capital into the public sector, the loss of international reserves ($3.2 billion) would have been even greater. To a large extent, foreign capital inflows to the public sector were made possible by a favorable international financial environment and extensive support from multilateral financial organizations.

Private Markets and Public Institutions

Together with a swift domestic policy response, the external financial support obtained by the authorities was key in preventing an economic collapse.[24] In effect, the sizable private capital outflow of the first nine months of the year (about U.S.$6.5 billion) was partially compensated for by inflows into the public sector. In the first six months of the year, these external resources came almost exclusively from international organizations and the specially tailored "Argentine bond."

In the second half of the year, once the worst of the crisis had passed, the public sector gained renewed access to voluntary private capital markets, albeit in the context of a rising country-risk premium. The return of the public sector to private capital markets served two purposes: it funded a process of debt restructuring, and it filled the gap between the originally estimated proceeds from privatization and tax revenues and the effective record.

Between August and December 1995, the public sector was able to raise a total of U.S.$4.4 billion in private international capital markets, to be followed by $1.9 billion in new issues during the first two months of 1996. Since November 1995, as internal conflicts subdued and the government announced the so-called second reform of the state, the price of Argentine assets boomed and spreads fell. As a result, for the first time in years, a $1 billion five-year global bond was issued in February 1996 with a spread over LIBOR (London Interbank Offered Rates) below that of a similar instrument issued by Mexico a few days before.

The renewed access of the public sector to private international capital markets after mid-1995 was made possible by a continuing relationship with international financial institutions, particularly the IMF. In effect, the authorities met IMF targets for the year, albeit with some cosmetics and the flexible compliance of the multilateral organization.

However, the deeper-than-expected recession had a severe impact on public sector revenues and the fiscal balance. The Argentine tax structure relies heavily on consumption taxes, which makes revenue collection extremely sensitive to the business cycle. In effect, in the January–October 1995 period, monthly tax collection fell 5.1 percent from the levels recorded one year earlier, with most of the contraction explained by the performance of value-added tax (VAT) revenues.[25] The disappointing tax revenue performance made the targets agreed on in March with the IMF unattainable, forcing a renegotiation. The new EFF targets convened in August were both more realistic and less demanding than those agreed to at the height of the crisis. The new agreement required the treasury not to exceed a U.S.$2.4 billion global deficit (before privatizations), as opposed to the $2 billion global surplus target negotiated in March. The August agreement also estimated a total of $1.2 billion from privatizations, with the gap to be financed by up to $1.2 billion in new debt.

The fiscal deficit for 1995 as a whole reached a total of U.S.$2.5 billion (excluding privatization proceeds), after a $1.5 billion primary surplus and $4.1 billion in interest payments. The imbalance was financed by $1.4 billion in new debt and $1.1 billion in privatization proceeds. This performance was eventually approved by the IMF even though the deficit was slightly above the agreed target. Furthermore, the IMF agreed to count as current receipts $1.35 billion in bank loans advanced to the government on behalf of future revenues from a tax and social security moratorium.

In a context in which relations with the IMF remain of paramount importance to maintaining access to international financial markets, in February 1996, the government and the IMF staff announced an understanding for a new twenty-one-month standby agreement (to be in force until December 1997), to start immediately after the expiration of the EFF in March 1996. The new agreement commits the government to a balanced budget for 1996, including up to U.S.$2.5 billion in capital revenues. But

this agreement is unlikely to make a significant direct contribution to the
external financial requirements of Argentina: the maximum amounts allowed by the quota have already been used so that disbursements will
likely equal amortizations.

The fact that Argentina was able to endure the fallout from the Mexican crisis without a major economic collapse has turned into an asset for
the government in its negotiations with international financial institutions
and even major creditor governments. By the same token, after the Mexican fiasco international financial institutions, and even the U.S. Treasury,
may not be willing to face a new major financial crisis. Although two set-
backs in a row is probably more than what the (private and public) financial community in Washington would like to witness, there is no question
that an emergency assistance program such as that mobilized for Mexico
will not be forthcoming in the event of a new crisis in Argentina. Flexibility and preemptive cooperation thus seems most likely.

Where Does Argentina Go from Here?

After the Mexican devaluation, Argentine authorities succeeded in preventing the worst-case scenario: financial collapse and an unmanageable
foreign exchange crisis. This took place pari passu with the maintenance
of the Convertibility Plan, the cornerstone of Argentine stabilization policy since 1991. Not only this, but the economic performance of Argentina
in the first year after the Mexican crisis compared favorably with that of
Mexico: real investment and output fell at a slower rate, the degree of financial distress was considerably lower than in Mexico, and the unemployment rate (although higher in absolute terms in Argentina than in
Mexico) showed a larger increase in Mexico.[26]

These divergences in short-run performance occurred even though the
external support Argentina received was considerably more modest than
that channeled to Mexico.[27] Argentina's comparatively better performance
can be explained by differences both in economic fundamentals and in
government response. As far as fundamentals are concerned, Argentina
displayed a relatively more solid fiscal stance than Mexico, more consistent monetary and exchange rate policies, and a lower external imbalance.
In effect, in 1994, the fiscal deficit (as a share of GDP) was higher in Mexico, even though public spending (particularly guarantees) was generally
accepted to be underreported. Similarly, in Mexico during 1994, the political cycle had led to overtly inconsistent monetary and exchange rate policies. Partly as a result, the Mexican current-account deficit (as a share of
GDP) doubled that of Argentina.

Different government responses were also a factor. Some observers
have regarded the Argentine record of 1995 as a vindication of "monetary
virtue," that is, of the superior ability of rules to cope with the effects of

expectational shocks. Others, including those who think that the worst is still ahead, regard it as the transient by-product of an eminently archaic policy regime.

Yet the Argentine government's response did not completely lack discretion. Although the maintenance of the fixed exchange rate regime was the cornerstone of official policy, monetary authorities managed the financial turmoil with more flexibility than it would appear at first sight. To a certain extent, management of the strains in the banking sector was discretionary and influenced by the electoral calendar. In effect, the authorities tried to minimize the number of bank closures to prevent a crisis of confidence and, in a preelectoral context, any concomitant political damage. During the first half of the year, they therefore intervened in financial markets to prop up liquidity and prevent a collapse of the payments chain. Discretion was limited, however, by the need to maintain the basic convertibility ratios. It is widely accepted that this flexibility prevented the financial turmoil to degenerate into a major banking crisis.

The Argentine government's faithful adherence to a fixed nominal exchange rate and full convertibility rule was remarkable in a preelectoral context, particularly because of its fiscal implications (a tough fiscal adjustment). Yet, rather than a vindication of monetary virtue per se, the government's response seems to have been the result of a shared conviction about the ineffectiveness of discretionary monetary and exchange rate policies in the specific circumstances of Argentina (an extensively dollarized financial system and a credibility problem).[28] Thus, monetary impotence rather than monetary virtue seems to have been the key factor behind official policies.

The recession that followed the Mexican crisis was very severe indeed. Real output contracted by an estimated 3–4 percent and real investment fell by 15.9 percent. The unemployment rate, in turn, reached a record level of 18.4 percent in May 1995 to fall to 16.4 percent in October. Coping with the recession has thus turned into an overriding economic priority. But the instruments available to pursue countercyclical economic policies are very limited. On the one hand, most of the flexibility to follow expansionary monetary policies were exhausted during the early phases of the crisis. On the other hand, fiscal expansionism is out of the question: although the budget deficit (as a share of GDP) is still low by international standards, financing that gap in capital markets cannot be taken for granted. Fiscal policy also seems trapped in the vicious circle of low economic activity, falling tax revenues, and widening budget imbalances.

Restoring Economic Growth

For the time being, the growth pattern typical of the 1991–1994 period seems to have ended. Conditions in international capital markets have changed, and sustained growth in the future will have to follow an invest-ment/export-led growth pattern. In the present circumstances, this longer-term challenge is exacerbated by the urgencies posed by the need to take the Argentine economy out of recession.

Indeed, the economy may settle into a low aggregate demand equilib-rium, one that may be economically and politically difficult to sustain in the medium term. On the one hand, investment spending is unlikely to re-cover fast unless aggregate demand reacts forcefully. Yet it is hard to see why the latter may happen. Budget constraints inhibit the public sector from using fiscal policy as a countercyclical device, while net exports are unlikely to continue to make as large a contribution as they did in 1995. If the rate of export growth returns to more sustainable one-digit rates, the still relatively low export/GDP ratio will limit the potential impact of net export growth on real GDP, at least in the short term.[29]

Consumption spending can hardly be expected to make a significant contribution to a fast recovery either. Low real incomes, high unemploy-ment, and the exhaustion of pent-up demand for consumer durables sug-gest that consumers' spending is unlikely to experience a sharp rebound. Furthermore, a credit-based recovery is unlikely: consumers seem reluc-tant to incur new debt. Indeed, these factors may pose a limit to economic growth even before a deterioration of the trade and current-account bal-ances act as a constraint on aggregate domestic demand growth.

The problems posed by the stagnant or slow-growth scenario are three-fold, one political and two economic. As regards the political constraint, it is uncertain whether the Argentine polity will tolerate two-digit levels of unemployment as a "long-run" feature of the economy. Even though growth is no guarantee of a rapid drop in unemployment rates, a continuing reces-sion or slow growth will certainly help keep unemployment rates high and may be politically disruptive. Furthermore, high unemployment may con-strain some of the very reform policies the government needs to deal with other pressing matters (such as adjustment in the provinces).

The two economic constraints refer to the fiscal and financial impli-cations of the stagnant or low-growth scenario. As for the former, since the structure of the tax system makes government revenues extremely sensi-tive to the business cycle, a low level of economic activity is difficult to reconcile with a balanced budget. Even though the imbalance is not sig-nificant (as a share of GDP), financing cannot be taken for granted. Fur-thermore, as of 1997, larger volumes of public sector debt will fall due, raising public sector gross borrowing requirements. Eventually, the fiscal constraint may even conflict with some of the government's structural re-forms (such as the overhaul of the pension and retirement system and the reduction in employer payroll taxes). Government spending and tax policy seem, therefore, a key area for future action.

The persistence of a recessionary environment may also counter a sus-tained improvement in the health of the financial system. A protracted recession may further deteriorate the quality of banks' assets and, given the regulatory constraints posed by convertibility, eventually reestablish a confidence problem. Although the government has taken steps to improve the system's liquidity and reduce systemic risks, what their contribution will be in the event of a confidence crisis is uncertain.

Relative Prices and External Fragility

The second problem, not completely isolated from the previous one, relates to the issue of competitiveness and the sustainability of external balance. As pointed out before, the relative prices issue came to the forefront during the expansionary phase of the Convertibility Plan, as the fixed nominal exchange rate and the persistence of a positive gap between the domestic and international inflation rates led to a real appreciation of the domestic currency. To partially counteract this trend and raise the real exchange rate, a number of policy decisions (such as the removal of distortive taxes and the deregulation of domestic markets) were implemented. These reinforced the increase in productivity brought about by the opening of the economy to foreign competition and the restructuring of the private sector.

Since external finance will not be as forthcoming in the future as in the past, the burden of adjustment will concentrate on the trade balance. This turns into key issues the questions of how significant the "exchange rate (relative prices) problem" is and how it can best be dealt with. Rapid export growth during 1995 was partly the result of factors such as higher international commodity prices, the demand "boom" in Brazil, and the depreciation of the dollar vis-à-vis other currencies. Although these factors are eminently transient, other more permanent changes have also been at play. In particular, productivity has increased significantly economy-wide.

There is no clear answer to whether the present structure of relative prices is capable of sustaining an export-led growth path in the future, because a lot will depend on the external environment. Yet it is interesting to note that there is a shared consensus that any remaining "relative prices problem" is unlikely to be solved in the foreseeable future by a nominal devaluation. Indeed, it may create even more strains and therefore be a last-resort action faced with a major (political and economic) crisis. But one thing is certain: preventing a further deterioration of relative prices in the context of a fixed nominal exchange rate will demand a slow growth of domestic aggregate demand in the years to come.

Conclusions

Although many of the problems are not new, the Argentine economy after the Mexican crisis is at a crossroads. To a certain extent, future performance will depend on the international environment. If capital markets are reluctant to provide external financing at a reasonable cost (even in the relatively modest amounts that would fuel growth in the Argentine economy at moderate rates), the automatic adjustment mechanisms of the Convertibility Plan will keep the economy in recession (or even take it into deflation). The latter, in turn, may further weaken the financial sector, the public sector balance, and the demand for labor.

If a more favorable external environment prevails, a more benign scenario can be envisaged, yet hardly one that would produce euphoria. Significant policy challenges remain ahead, many of which will demand maturity, cooperation, and flexibility on the part of the Argentine polity.

The depth of the economic crisis of the 1980s helps explain the radical policy choices made in Argentina since the early 1990s, in particular the adoption of a currency board mechanism to combat inflation, improved expectations, and enforced discipline in the public sector. It is generally accepted that under normal conditions the rigidity of a policy regime is a handicap: the more limited the number of instruments available, the lower the number of independent policy objectives that can be pursued by the authorities. In such a context, policy dilemmas and trade-offs multiply. Yet conditions have not been normal in Argentina for many years now.

In the 1991–1994 period, the Convertibility Plan proved to be a powerful instrument for coping with inflation, improving expectations, and enforcing fiscal discipline in the public sector. Similarly, after the Mexican crisis, maintaining the Convertibility Plan allowed Argentina to avoid the worst-case scenario. But the long-term prospects for the Argentine economy cannot be deduced from this record. In effect, the long-term success of the Convertibility Plan will be measured by its ability to again base anti-inflationary policies on monetary and income policies instead of the exchange rate. Such a policy mix would free the exchange rate to be targeted to output and employment objectives, and would relieve fiscal policy from being the only instrument to achieve a change in relative prices and resource transfers.

From a practical standpoint, however, the key question is whether in the present context the rigidities of the Convertibility Plan reflect genuine policy preferences or the simple acceptance of the limits to monetary and exchange rate discretion still imposed by past experience. Sustained economic growth is likely to demand more than a currency board. But providing an answer in Argentina will be no easy task.

Notes

1. I thank Hernán Soltz for his able research assistance. Juan Carlos Barboza, Clint Smith, and Riordan Roett made useful comments to a preliminary version of

this chapter. I am also grateful to Wendy Campbell for her editorial work. Responsibility for any remaining errors is mine.

2. See Paul Krugman, "Monetary Virtue Leads Two-Peso Tussle," *Financial Times,* June 13, 1995.

3. For an overview of the effects of and policy response to the debt crisis, see Roberto Bouzas, "Beyond Stabilization and Reform," in R. Bouzas et al., *In the Shadow of Debt* (New York: Twentieth Century Fund, 1992).

4. As a result, between 1989 and 1994 privatization rendered the government about U.S.$10 billion in cash and more than $14 billion in debt reduction.

5. For a discussion, see Pablo Gerchunoff and José Luis Machinea, "Un ensayo sobre política económica después de la estabilización," in P. Bustos, ed., *Más allá de la estabilidad* (Buenos Aires: Fundación Friedrich Ebert, 1995).

6. During 1994, the CPI and WPI increased by 3.9 and 5.9 percent, respectively.

7. Furthermore, tax collection—centered on a value-added tax—became extremely sensitive to the level of economic activity.

8. Following the so-called *Pacto de Olivos* between the Peronist and Radical leaderships, in December 1993, congress passed legislation declaring the need to reform the 1853 constitution. Delegates to the constituent assembly were elected in April 1994. The most significant outcomes of the reform were to reduce the presidential term from six to four years and to allow reelection for one additional term (a benefit also conferred on President Menem).

9. In 1994, the public sector deficit was equivalent to 0.36 percent of GDP, in contrast to a 0.81 surplus posted in the previous year.

10. A major issue of dispute was the IMF's demand to increase taxes. The anticipated conclusion of the agreement also saved the government from a renegotiation of targets with the IMF in a preelectoral period.

11. Investment rates also rose faster in Argentina. Between 1991 and 1994, the investment rate (as a share of GDP) increased by 2.1 and 5.9 percentage points, respectively, in Mexico and Argentina. The sharp rise in the latter took place from the very depressed levels of 1990.

12. The central bank's international reserve figures exclude dollar-denominated treasury bills.

13. With the benefit of hindsight, the swift policy response contributed to the administration's electoral success in the May elections.

14. The new charter approved in 1992 prohibited the central bank from acting as a lender of last resort. There was no deposit insurance scheme in operation either.

15. Congress endorsed the reform some weeks later. "Excess reserves" are those above minimum convertibility ratios.

16. Trust funds would be endowed with a total of U.S.$5 billion from the proceeds of the foreign and domestic tranches of the so-called Argentine bond (see next note) and loans from the World Bank and the Inter-American Development Bank.

17. The "Argentine bond" was a U.S.$2 billion bond floated among domestic and external institutional investors at a discount over Argentine market yields at the time. Its successful subscription was regarded as an indicator of the private sector's support of official policies. The external support package amounted to a total of U.S.$8.2 billion.

18. The February 1995 package was designed to cut expenditures by U.S.$1.0 billion and increase revenues by $2.0 billion. On that occasion the government expected to restore a primary surplus sufficient to pay all interest due in 1995 (estimated to reach $4.0 billion).

19. The value-added tax was increased for one year from 18 to 21 percent, a 3 percent import statistical surcharge was reestablished, export rebates were cut by one-fourth, and employer social security contributions for industry, agriculture, tourism, and scientific research (originally reduced as part of the fiscal measures taken in 1993–1994) were increased by 30 percent.

20. Examples include the special labor regime for small and medium-sized firms and minor reforms to the social security system.

21. In 1989, hyperinflation and economic collapse were fueled by fears that the winning party might embark on irresponsible economic policies (the so-called productive revolution and the *salariazo*). Yet immediately after taking office, President Menem made a U-turn toward conventional economic stabilization and reform policies.

22. Some analysts referred to a so-called installment vote (fear of a devaluation from dollar-indebted households and firms) as a factor in Menem's victory. Yet the installment vote most likely influenced the stance of the opposition as well.

23. In the first half of 1995, the share of the ten largest banks in total deposits jumped from 50.6 to 58.1 percent. The share of dollar-denominated deposits in total deposits also increased by more than 3 percentage points.

24. The U.S.$8 billion external support package obtained by Argentina in March 1995 was much lower than the $47.6 billion the Clinton administration put together to assist Mexico in February 1995.

25. Although the VAT rate increased from 18 to 21 percent in March 1995, VAT total collection remained stable as a result of the downturn in economic activity. Social security taxes also fell, due to higher evasion and falling real incomes.

26. Preliminary estimates indicate that real GDP fell by 6.9 and 3.5–4.0 percent in Mexico and Argentina, respectively, during 1995. The financial distress Mexico experienced after the devaluation of the peso was also considerably greater than that of Argentina as measured, for example, by the rise of real interest rates or the share of nonperforming loans in total bank assets.

27. Of course, the sizable package put together by the Clinton administration to assist Mexico was an indirect factor in the ensuing performance of Argentina. The Mexican rescue operation served to limit damage on other economies, which may have suffered even more if Mexico had defaulted on its external commitments.

28. Furthermore, in contrast to Argentina, about a third of Mexico's public sector liabilities were due within a year. This explains the sizable external support required to prevent the default of the Mexican public sector.

29. In 1995, when the value of merchandise exports expanded by 31.9 percent and imports fell by 7.5 percent, net exports contributed only 1.3 percentage points to total GDP growth.

6

Repercussions of the Mexican Monetary Crisis Across the Atlantic: Ripples, Breakers, or a Sea Change in European Perspectives?

Wolf Grabendorff[1]

Mexico's current financial crisis was triggered on December 20, 1994, by a badly handled devaluation of the peso and plummeting external investor confidence. The underlying economic and political causes of the crisis were several. The peso had been significantly overvalued during President Carlos Salinas de Gortari's final year in office, which in turn hindered exports and encouraged imports, damaged important sectors of the domestic economy, and led to a massive and rising current-account deficit (equivalent to 8 percent of gross domestic product, or GDP, in 1994).[2] Meanwhile, Mexico had entered perhaps its worst period of political instability since the 1920s. The January 1994 outbreak of the Chiapas rebellion, which continued throughout the year, and the assassination of Luis Donaldo Colosio, the original presidential candidate of the Institutional Revolutionary Party (PRI), on March 23, 1994, and of José Francisco Ruiz Massieu, the party's secretary-general, on September 28, 1994, all compounded the unsettled political atmosphere that is otherwise normal at the end of a presidential *sexenio*.

In Europe, as in the Americas and elsewhere, many observers had long expected a change of course in Mexican economic policy management, as well as a devaluation of the Mexican peso. After all, several major European Union (EU) countries, including Great Britain, Italy, and Spain, had been forced to undergo painfully severe currency devaluations in the two years immediately preceding the outbreak of the peso crisis.[3] Yet few experts, if any, predicted the damage that would ultimately be wrought on the Mexican economy. Nor had they foreseen the "contagion effect" that the crisis would have on some other economies in the region and elsewhere.

In fact, the repercussions have ranged across the Atlantic as well, engendering a uniquely European perspective on the peso crisis, Latin America's reaction, and the position and strategy of the United States in the region, particularly with respect to the evolution of the North American Free Trade Agreement (NAFTA) and intrahemispheric integration in general. As one analyst has pointed out, "In Europe . . . worries about NAFTA becoming 'Fortress America' blurred the fact that one of the walls of the fortress had shaky foundations."[4]

The Outcome

The Mexican monetary crisis has engendered effects quite distinct from anything that the 1980s Latin American debt problem might have led us to expect. The economic outcome for the entire region has been singularly heterogenous, depending on the country in question or whether the focus is on capital flows as against real GDP performance. Moreover, at least in the Mexican case, the outcome of the crisis has been affected by the early and massive response of the international financial institutions. This is, in itself, a further crucial distinction from the early 1980s, when the International Monetary Fund (IMF) was the sole, and reluctant, international financial firefighter. Indeed, the Mexican crisis has had an impact on the multilateral institutions themselves, notably with respect to external perceptions about their future global roles. Moreover, events in Mexico have had a measurable, if indirect, economic impact on Europe—mainly transmitted through the exchange rate—as well as on Europeans' notions of their place in the new global economic framework.

Crisis Management in Mexico and the Rest of Latin America

Despite the severity of the peso crisis, most European observers agree that its *financial* repercussions are now largely under control, as is the associated contagion effect in Argentina and some other Latin American countries. In this sense, the current situation is remarkably different from Mexico's last major financial crisis, which started in August 1982 and which triggered a regional and international debt crisis, cut Latin America off from voluntary borrowing for the remainder of the decade, and for the most part ruined the entire region's growth prospects throughout the 1980s.

In January 1995, not even the most optimistic analysts predicted that Latin America would be able to return to the world capital markets in the second quarter of the year. International pessimism about the region's prospects evaporated almost as rapidly as it had set in after the peso crisis broke out. According to the latest estimates, from April to June 1995 Latin American governments successfully issued U.S.$5.2 billion in bonds on world markets by summer, a stunning recovery from the mere $200 million recorded for the preceding quarter. In fact, in the whole of last year, bond issuing was well above the average for 1994.[5] According to figures released in January 1996 by the Institute of International Finance, private capital flows to Latin America totaled $37 billion in 1995—and could reach $52 billion this year.[6]

A *Financial Times* editorial on August 7, 1995, stressed that Argentina's successful return to the international bond markets—alongside Brazil and Mexico—was an important milestone for Latin America and indicated that the currency virus had been short-lived from the perspective of the financial markets. Other commentaries emphasized the fact that the two countries worst affected by the peso crisis have been able to return to the international markets. In the second quarter of 1995, Argentina raised U.S.$1.6 billion, and Mexico, $500 million. Experts have attributed their recovery to

- The huge U.S.-coordinated international rescue package for Mexico (which eventually totaled some $50 billion in external commitments)
- Intervention by the International Monetary Fund and the World Bank to support Argentina's fixed-parity exchange rate[7]
- The fact that Brazil's currency, the *real*—and the Brazilian economy as a whole—was spared the worst of the contagion[8]
- Efforts in Argentina, Brazil, and Mexico to keep economic liberalization policy on course, and indeed to speed it up (particularly with respect to privatization and other measures to stimulate domestic and foreign direct investment)

Yet one should be careful to distinguish between renewed capital flows and any perceived recovery in domestic GDP. Mexico's economy shrank by at least 4 percent in 1995.[9] Mexican President Ernesto Zedillo has remained optimistic, after stating on July 27, 1995, that after seven months of discipline, the crisis seemed to be abating and Mexico could look forward to economic growth again in 1996. As a result of booming exports, Mexico ended the year with a U.S.$7.4 billion trade surplus—the first time it had moved out of deficit since 1989.[10] He pointed to a $2.6 billion trade surplus in the first six months of 1995, generated by a 32 percent increase in exports from the same period in 1994; a falling monthly inflation rate; and Mexico's having largely met its obligations to holders of *tesobonos,* the short-term dollar-denominated bonds that were coming due when the crisis hit in December.[11] But independent analysts have remained cautious.[12]

Of particular concern are the continued weakness of the Mexican banking system, spiraling unemployment (over 400,000 Mexicans lost their jobs in the first half of 1995), and weak consumer demand and continued high indebtedness among companies and households.[13] Also in question is the underlying strength of Mexico's export-led recovery. Although exports have soared, many analysts expected an even steeper rise, since the peso was trading at barely half of its peak value. Given the depth of the current economic crisis, Mexico is likely to face continuing difficulty for at least the next eighteen months.

Growth has also been way below expectations in Argentina, the country (after Mexico) hardest hit by the contagion effect. Figures released by the Instituto Nacional de Estadísticas y Censos (INEC) in December 1995 indicate that Argentine output fell by 2.5 percent last year, although GDP should rise by around 2 percent in 1996. The Argentine economy will need time to recover its precrisis output and employment trends and expectations. Unemployment, for example, rose to a record 18.6 percent by mid-1995.[14] Nevertheless, economic recovery should be boosted by exports. According to INEC data, Argentina registered a $1 billion trade surplus in the first ten months of 1995, as against a $4.8 billion deficit in the same period last year.

Moreover, the longer-term GDP prospects for Mexico, Argentina, and other Latin American countries are considerably brighter. A recent projection exercise by the World Bank indicated that Latin American and Caribbean nations have the potential to double their average growth rate to 6 percent annually over the next decade. The World Bank regards the common policy response to the Mexican crisis—namely, deepening the existing economic reforms—as a major reason such steep growth can be expected.[15]

Crisis Management by the International Financial Institutions

The peso crisis has markedly altered EU perceptions of the role of multilateral institutions. Early on, senior financial officials in EU member states had expressed anger over U.S. pressure to support the international rescue package for Mexico. Belgium, Germany, the Netherlands, Norway, Switzerland, and the United Kingdom all abstained from the February 1, 1995, vote in the IMF Board of Governors to approve a U.S.$18.9 billion contribution to the Mexico rescue package.[16] All told, those European abstainers represented over 25 percent of IMF voting capital.[17]

EU finance ministers subsequently put on a public show of consensus with the United States at the February 3–4, 1995, summit of the Group of Seven (G-7) in Toronto, expressing support for Washington's economic plan for Mexico. Statements to that effect were issued by Lamberto Dini, the Italian treasury minister, and by Theo Waigel, the German finance minister.[18] Nevertheless, an underlying resentment remains.

Lingering EU objections concern both the package itself and its presentation as a fait accompli. The main objection is that the United States has used European money to pursue its own policy objectives in Mexico. Waigel said immediately before the Toronto summit that Germany wished that consultation coordination had been better.[19] German policymakers believed the sums involved in the package were too high, and that it was carried out too rapidly. Indeed, EU officials were not convinced that Mexico's difficulties would spill over into some kind of "true, world endemic crisis" if not immediately dealt with—the view held by the Clinton administration, by Alan Greenspan, chairman of the U.S. Federal Reserve, and by IMF president Michel Camdessus.[20] Instead, the dominant views in the EU were:

- Mexico's financial turmoil was part of a necessary, and overdue, correction of financial institutions' overly optimistic assessments of the risks of investing in an emerging market.
- The large losses suffered by financial institutions holding Mexican bonds did not pose a global threat—nor, in fact, would similar difficulties in a number of other developing countries.
- Although serious losses by large commercial banks might indeed threaten a global debacle, the difference between Mexico's current crisis and the events of August 1982 (which precipitated the global debt crisis) is precisely the relatively small role played by banks this time around.
- A separate, but no less important, concern was that the massive rescue plan posed a "moral hazard" that might encourage precisely the kind of behavior that *would* launch a systemic crisis. In other words, investors would be tempted to overextend themselves in risky investments, confident that the industrialized countries would bail them out of any liquidity problems—a sure way to render the world financial system fragile indeed.

Certainly, as an indirect result of the Mexican crisis, those EU currencies most closely linked to the U.S. dollar (particularly the Spanish peseta and the British pound) did drop in value as a result of the turbulence in the foreign exchange markets. As a logical counterpart, the deutsche mark and its shadow currencies rose in value. That externally generated currency volatility strained intra-EU economic relations as well. It distorted internal trade flows by curbing the exports of those with the hardest currencies (the deutsche mark bloc) by boosting those of the softer money countries (Italy, Portugal, Spain, and the United Kingdom), and thus compounding fears of "competitive devaluations" among EU member states.[21] Moreover, the volatility also disrupted the EU's system of "green currencies," used to determine payments to member states' farmers under the Common Agricultural Policy. The Mexican shock waves have therefore had their greatest impact across the Atlantic in the difficult process of adjusting European monetary policy—in line with the broader goal of achieving economic and monetary union (EMU) by 1999.

The Strategies

The earlier-than-expected recovery of international capital flows to Latin America and the reasonable (given the circumstances) growth prospects in the region for 1996 onward tend to obscure some wider repercussions of the Mexican financial crisis. Most important, the United States and Europe have parted ways in their views of how to deal with the Mexican predicament (as has been the case with other major international issues in recent years). The peso crisis shifted both the U.S. and the EU approaches to Latin America, albeit in very divergent ways.

A Changing U.S. Strategy Toward Its Hemispheric Neighbors

The Mexican financial crisis has had a marked impact on both policymakers and public opinion in the United States. A seeming retrenchment from the ever expanding liberalization of trade witnessed before the crisis can be traced to two sources. One was the initial but then extended clamor over giving Mexico such a large amount of financial support from public funds. Significant opposition still exists in the U.S. Congress (on both sides of the aisle) to continued disbursements from the $20 billion emergency fund set up by the U.S. Treasury. Not only is the fund viewed as excessively large, but its basis is contingency monies set aside for other purposes. A second source of retrenchment is the recognition of the direct repercussions of the crisis for the U.S. economy. Since January 1995, the crisis seems to have demonstrated that significant trade liberalization between unequal economic partners is risky not only for the weaker party:

- The crisis slowed U.S. exports to Mexico and greatly boosted Mexican sales in the United States during 1995; Mexico ran an U.S.$8.4 billion surplus on bilateral trade in the first half of the year, with a similar surplus in the latter half.[22]
- The crisis has also affected the U.S. dollar, which in early 1995 hit postwar lows against the Japanese yen and fell badly against the stronger European currencies, particularly the deutsche mark, thereby increasing inflationary pressures from rising prices for imports.

As a result, many in Congress and even in the Clinton administration itself have grown wary of pursuing further hemisphere-wide free-trade initiatives. This reluctance is a potentially serious obstacle to extending NAFTA to the Free Trade Area of the Americas (FTAA) initiative: President Clinton has yet to ask Congress for a "fast track" to negotiate Chile's joining NAFTA (whose parties extended the invitation to do so in December 1994) and, presumably, to cover other inter-American trade accords as well. If the president failed to make his request by the end of 1995, the presidential election campaign of 1996 will inevitably delay matters beyond 1997. As Moisés Naím, an analyst of U.S. policy, has noted: "At a time in which half of world trade takes place under preferential conditions among members of regional trading arrangements, the Mexican crash has pushed the prospect for extending NAFTA to the rest of the hemisphere until well into the next century."[23]

But greater U.S. caution (or, at the very least, a "pause for breath") over trade liberalization in the Western Hemisphere stands in stark contrast to Washington's much more aggressive and coherent strategy to raise the U.S. profile in Latin American markets. A revised strategy to promote U.S. exports and investments to the south was first set out on January 9, 1995, by Jeffrey Garten, then U.S. undersecretary of commerce for international trade.[24]

The Garten strategy involves the use of a wide range of tools to promote inter-American commerce: cabinet-level business development missions, specific target contracts selected by trade officials, pressures by diplomatic delegations abroad, credits from federal financial agencies such as the Export-Import Bank, the threat of retaliatory action using Section 301 of the Omnibus Trade Act (against "unfair" competition), and new export assistance centers to help small- and medium-sized U.S. enterprises. This strategy has been focused on a cluster of high-growth industries in the big emerging markets: information, environmental, transportation, energy, and health care technologies and financial services. According to Garten, the Clinton administration is not the first to assist U.S. companies in winning markets, but it is the first to mount such an aggressive and systematic export promotion strategy. He has noted that policymakers' motives for fostering U.S. commerce are chiefly economic (as befits the post–Cold War era) and are, from Washington's perspective, logical:

- From 1987 to 1994, exports of goods and services accounted for over 33 percent of U.S. GNP growth.
- Export-related employment grew eight times faster than total U.S. employment (accounting for almost all net job creation in manufacturing).
- Workers in the export-oriented manufacturing sector earn 13 percent more, on average, than workers in U.S. manufacturing as a whole.[25]

These points are all the more relevant given the following reasons. First, U.S. sales in Latin America have risen by an average of 20.5 percent annually over the past five years, making the region the fastest-growing market in the world for U.S. exports. Such sales totaled U.S.$82 billion in 1994 alone. Moreover, official projections indicate that by 2010, exports to Latin America will have risen 190 percent (to $232 billion annually) and will exceed the nation's exports to the EU by $100 billion a year. Although EU exports to Latin America are also rising quickly (up an average of 14 percent yearly since 1990), their rate of increase has not matched the U.S. rate, and thus the United States is the one increasing its relative market share in the region.[26]

Second, U.S. investment in Latin America is also large and growing fast. The region now receives some 60 percent of all U.S. foreign direct investment (FDI) in the developing world. Inflows of U.S. investment rose by a stunning 140 percent from 1990 to 1993 (reaching $9 billion in the latter year). In the first four years of the 1990s, the United States supplied three-quarters of all foreign direct investment in Latin America, and the EU less than a quarter. In fact, EU flows in 1993 were barely $1.9 billion, some 6.5 percent below the figure for 1990. Japanese foreign direct investment in the region plunged even more, to only $15 million in 1993.[27]

The Mexican crisis, with its direct consequences for the U.S. economy, will strengthen the case for such "trade advocacy" (also referred to by Garten as the "National Export Strategy"), but at the expense of formal trade liberalization agreements. The Clinton administration now sees expanding advantages from a coherent approach designed to force open the big emerging markets in Latin America and Asia (only for U.S. exports and investment), while employing a range of commercial weapons to beat off potential challenges from EU nations and Japan.

With this stance, the administration is calculating that it can reap considerable economic rewards *despite* only slow progress toward NAFTA expansion and the FTAA. Proper trade liberalization agreements would, in fact, mean reciprocal access and advantages for Latin America, implying real or perceived domestic costs for the United States. Aggressive trade advocacy is a much more one-sided route to the same basic U.S. economic objectives, and it indicates that Washington is girding for a unilateral, as opposed to multilateral, approach to world commerce. Another such indicator is the U.S. government's decision not to join the global agreement on financial services signed on July 26, 1995, by some ninety countries (including Japan and the Asian newly industrialized countries), which is estimated to cover 90 percent of world trade in these services. Tellingly, the agreement was the first major international commercial accord since World War II to have gone ahead despite a refusal by the United States to take part.

Latin American Reactions to the Contagion Effect

From the European perspective, the current brakes on NAFTA expansion and the FTAA actually brighten the prospects for Mercosur (the Southern Cone Common Market, established in August 1994 by Argentina, Brazil, Paraguay, and Uruguay) and for intra–South American integration in general. Brazil is regarded as the key player in these developments, particularly because the two chief external goals of the new administration of Fernando Henrique Cardoso are to consolidate the Mercosur customs union and free-trade area and to establish regional foreign policy and trade leadership through the South American Free Trade Area (ALCAS). The latter would be a de facto extension of Mercosur, individually or by negotiations between the Mercosur and Andean Pact signatories. Southern Cone integration is already gathering pace: Bolivia will join Mercosur in July 1996; and Chile, while rejecting full membership, seeks an "association agreement."[28]

The basic goal of ALCAS is to advance toward the liberalization of substantially all intraregional trade (at least 80 percent) via automatically scheduled reductions of tariffs from 1995 to 2005. Argentina has already offered support for ALCAS, and the Mercosur and Andean Pact nations have already initiated a series of discussions on how to establish closer economic links. Over the medium term, the two integration schemes, both of which are now official customs unions and free-trade areas, could begin to converge. Indeed, the ALCAS concept basically calls for a fusion of the Mercosur and the Andean Pact partners, since together they include all the main South American economies except Chile.[29]

The view from Europe is not just that South American integration is bound to proceed without the United States, but also that U.S. policymakers may ultimately lend at least tacit support to Brazil's goal of consolidating a South American economic space, for several reasons:

- The consolidation would give the United States time to prepare for hemispheric trade liberalization, without losing out on export and investment opportunities.
- The impetus of economic integration would be allowed to continue in Latin America.
- The whole FTAA process would thereby be made simpler, with fewer building blocs involved.

It is important to stress that this view covers only *South American* integration. The peso crisis has made Mexico a less attractive integration partner for Central America and other regions. The key factor here is the trade-distorting effect of a cheap peso in a context of free-trade agreements (FTAs)—for example, with Costa Rica, Colombia, and Venezuela. Another, more general, factor is that any northern bloc covering the greater Caribbean area would be much more heavily influenced by the United States than a southern bloc (ALCAS), because of both structural factors (trade, investment, and technology flows) and "push and pull" factors between a powerful economy and its weaker neighbors.[30] The United States has shown a preference for bilateral FTAs over broader economic integration. And given the Mexican crisis, Washington may tilt even farther away from FTAs.

EU Strategy Toward Latin America

Although the Mexican crisis has occasioned in EU policymakers a concern for some short-term caution with respect to trade liberalization agreements with Latin America, their perspectives on the needed Latin American response in the longer term—to speed up regional integration—have, in turn, influenced European strategy toward the region. Principally, the result has been a general confirmation of the long-term EU goal of strengthening relations with Latin America and Southeast Asia for strictly economic reasons. Since the crisis erupted, the EU has continued its active trade and investment strategy toward Latin America's big emerging markets, which was first developed and articulated in early 1994. Progress is still being made on a series of negotiations, or draft negotiating briefs, for accords with Mercosur, Mexico, and Chile:

- Just two days after the peso crisis broke, the EU Council of Ministers and the European Commission issued with Mercosur a joint declaration on forthcoming negotiations over an interregional agreement.
- On February 8, 1995, the European Commission proposed closer EU-Mexico links through an agreement on economic cooperation and political consultation comparable to that between the EU and Mercosur.
- On April 10, the Council of Ministers approved a European Commission strategy for future relations with Mexico and asked the commission to propose directives for negotiating a new political, commercial, and economic accord during 1995.
- On May 2 Alain Juppé, acting president of the Council of Ministers; Manuel Marín, vice-president of the European Commission; and José Angel Gurría, foreign minister of Mexico, signed a joint declaration on the intention to negotiate an EU-Mexico agreement and the procedures for the negotiations.
- On June 12, the Council of Ministers adopted a negotiating directive for the interregional agreement with Mercosur.
- On July 17, 1995, the Council of Ministers approved a strategy for a comparable bilateral agreement with Chile, asking the European Commission to submit a draft negotiating directive.

The EU agreements with Mercosur, Mexico, and Chile will all involve

- A gradual, reciprocal deregulation of trade in goods and services (and investment), taking account of the sensitivity of some products for either or both parties, and conducted in accordance with the rules of the World Trade Organization (WTO)—though in the Mercosur case, a full trade accord will not be signed until at least the year 2000
- Political dialogue at the technical, ministerial, and presidential levels

- An intensification of cooperation, particularly on the environment, information technology, services, and science and technology[31]

Manuel Marín has stressed that despite Mexico's problems, the EU will seek to strengthen political and economic ties with the region. There will be intense negotiations on the new agreements with Mexico and Chile during the Italian presidency of the EU, which ends in 1996. The EU-Mercosur framework agreement was initialed by the relevant parties on September 29, 1995, in Montevideo and signed at the December 15–16, 1995, European Council in Madrid. Marín believes that the negotiating directive for Mexico should be viewed as an indication of the EU's commitment— indeed, as an "act of conviction."[32] In fact, during 1996 the EU will be involved in simultaneous negotiations with the (wider) Mercosur, Mexico, Chile, and Cuba (on the initial framework of a cooperation accord), as well as with the Andean and Central American countries (on new subregional commercial and cooperation agreements).[33]

Clearly, the EU is seeking to secure access to the most dynamic markets of the next century. Its strategy does, however, appear to involve the proviso of a "safety period." In the Mercosur case, a trade liberalization agreement will be signed only some five years *after* the interregional "economic and cooperation" accord. The net result will be to postpone the onset of EU-Mercosur trade liberalization until around the year 2001. All told, the delay will give the EU a de facto fifteen-year transition period for its most sensitive products—without appearing to break the new GATT/WTO rules. These stipulate that "substantially all" trade must be liberalized within ten years (i.e., by January 1, 2005, *if* a free trade agreement had actually been signed in 1995). Since freer commerce with Mexico and Chile is perceived by Europe as less risky, the respective agreements will incorporate trade liberalization provisions.

It is important to note, nevertheless, that the concept of a safety period was *not* induced by the Mexican crisis, having been drawn up well before then. If EU commercial strategy toward Latin America experiences significant modifications in the short to medium term, it will be as a result of newly aggressive U.S. tactics—and not as a direct consequence of the Mexican financial crisis.

Lessons from the Mexican Peso Crisis

The Mexican peso crisis has led to increased discussion on whether the existing international financial institutions—such as the International Monetary Fund and the World Bank—are appropriately equipped to respond to today's global financial challenges. Questions emerge on how to provide new means to guarantee economic and monetary stability in a world of

increasingly globalized markets, particularly within the context of differing regional political and economic interests and priorities. The lessons
drawn from the Mexican crisis are thus useful in rethinking long-term
strategies, such as integration schemes versus free-trade areas.

International Financial Management and Institutions

Alain Juppé, subsequently appointed French prime minister, said in his
opening address at the fifth EU–Rio Group summit (held in Paris March
17–18, 1995) that the Mexican crisis should spur discussion of new means
to guarantee international economic and monetary stability. Manuel Marín
added that since markets have become globalized, their management must
also be globalized.[34] Such points are by no means a shared conviction in
the EU, however. Germany and the United Kingdom do not favor as inter-
ventionist an approach as that suggested by France, although both agree
that new monetary management instruments are necessary.

More specifically, largely at European insistence, the Toronto G-7
summit addressed the role of the IMF in future crises. France, Italy, and
the United Kingdom all stressed that the fund has to improve its control
mechanisms for developing countries, based on a concern that current IMF
(and World Bank) remedies are out of date for a global economy.

European observers believe that, despite the smiles at Toronto, the
problems of managing international economic policy coordination are
many, and thorny. The United States pushed through the rescue package
for Mexico out of self-interest, wanting to avoid political and economic
destabilization in Mexico (and associated spurs to emigrants) and to bail
out the primarily U.S. investment and insurance companies that were
worst affected by the peso crisis. U.S. investment in Mexico was mostly
portfolio flows, likely to be directly hit by the crisis. EU investment, however, was mainly direct investment and thus was affected by the financial
crisis less directly, for example, via reduced demand for the goods or services of investing firms. EU member states could thus justifiably argue
that the rescue package was designed explicitly to benefit U.S. firms much
more than their European counterparts.

The Mexican crisis and the U.S.-led response are regarded as further
symptoms rather than further causes of the diverging interests between key
European countries and the United States. The divergence has grown over
the past few years, for two reasons. First, the big emerging markets, which
are by definition outside the industrialized world, are becoming increasingly important within the global economy and will become more so since
they are growing at much faster rates than the developed nations. Yet there
is no forum in which the G-7 can meet and exchange information and
views with such markets as Argentina, Brazil, India, or Indonesia.[35] A key
issue on the EU–Rio Group agenda in the future will therefore be that of

a common biregional strategy for cooperation with respect to the roles and priorities of the international financial institutions. Second, large regional trading blocs have developed, most notably the EU and the NAFTA partners. Hence, regional priorities cut across G-7 ties. Free-flowing capital movements, an important part of globalization, strengthened those ties considerably more in the case of the United States and Mexico than in the case of the EU and the Central and Eastern European Countries (CEECs), the Mediterranean nations, and the African, Caribbean, and Pacific (ACP) countries.[36] Washington's response to the Mexican financial crisis—to construct a massive rescue package and expect support from EU and other nations—highlights Mexico's importance in the particular regional context of the United States.

Diverging EU and U.S. Interests

European observers have discerned a trend toward the "regionalization" of economic crisis management. This was not the case during the 1980s debt crisis, when the European governments, the United States, and the multilateral institutions were equally involved in trying to contain its effects on Latin America, Africa, and parts of Asia. Today, however, the U.S. administration seems to be further advanced along the regionalization road than the EU, even though the EU now plays an important role in structural adjustment programs for some ACP countries.

It is notable in this regard that the IMF rejected a U.S.$6.4 billion package for Russia just prior to its huge loan to Mexico, on the grounds that President Yeltsin's reforms were insufficient and that IMF funds might end up financing Russian military action (a suspicion confirmed by army intervention in Chechenya on December 11, 1994). EU policymakers agreed with that decision, despite the fact that they consider political and economic developments in Russia (especially its unstable leadership) to be of great "regional" importance. The Mexican bailout obliged the IMF to extend an assistance package seven times its normal limit, involving fully a fifth of its liquid assets. Had Russia received comparable terms, it would have been entitled to more than $40 billion from the IMF alone.[37]

Tough EU conditions on providing multilateral funds to Russia contrast sharply with Washington's eagerness to channel (partly European) money to Mexico—even though the EU and the United States are both cognizant of the political and economic interests at stake in their respective regions. It is therefore improbable that the EU would have attempted to organize an international rescue package on such a huge scale if, for example, a similar financial crisis had befallen a large neighbor such as Poland.

Some would argue that the differing responses to the Mexican financial crisis are simply further evidence of the divergence between U.S. and

EU strategies toward Latin America that are taking shape.[38] The Clinton administration has embraced the Garten strategy of aggressively pursuing U.S. commercial interests by all means available. The White House may be extending a similar principle to multilateral action, now that economic interests are at the fore of national security thinking. The EU's commercial strategy is different, featuring a cautious and carefully planned series of trade liberalization agreements with Latin America's big emerging markets—as well as generous preferential schemes for the less advanced countries—to ensure European commercial access to the region into the next century. Not surprisingly, therefore, the EU member states have not been so aggressive in the multilateral context.

Risk Reduction in Mexico and the Rest of Latin America

Practical lessons from the Mexican crisis cited by numerous senior EU officials—including Edmond Alphandery, French finance minister; Kenneth Clarke, U.K. chancellor of the exchequer; Eddie George, governor of the Bank of England; Hans Tietmeyer, president of the Bundesbank; and Theo Waigel, German finance minister—include the following:[39]

- Currencies such as the Mexican peso should be linked to the dollar or other major currencies only if domestic economic policies and circumstances so allow.
- International surveillance of the big emerging markets should be intensified, with a watch-list of "sensitive countries" under close scrutiny to ensure that any sudden drop in reserves (loss of liquidity) does not put them on the brink of bankruptcy.
- Multilateral institutions and the governments of the leading industrialized nations should avoid the moral hazard posed by extending massive rescue packages, which give countries less incentive to take the tough steps necessary to stabilize their economies.
- Currency crises require decisive management of planning, timing, and communication. (As noted elsewhere in this book, the Argentine and Brazilian economic policy teams scored better than their Mexican counterparts in this respect.)
- Better monitoring and faster coordination by the G-7, the IMF, and the World Bank are essential in the event of any future crises like the Mexican episode.

European analysts also stress that the Mexican crisis has implications for capital inflows. First, Argentina, Brazil, Mexico, and certain other Latin American nations have been able to resume borrowing on international capital markets only at the cost of much stricter conditionality; interest rate spreads are now significantly higher and maturity periods much shorter, averaging only two years, as opposed to around four years before the Mexican crisis.

Second, international markets are increasingly distinguishing the particular differences among Latin American countries—a major shift with respect to the debt crisis of the eighties, when all the region's borrowers were hit by the contagion effect.[40] Chile and Colombia are regarded as investment-grade countries and can thus raise longer-term financing (of five to six years) on the international capital markets.[41] Indeed, Chile is now receiving such large foreign investment inflows (projected to reach U.S.$5 billion for 1995, or around 10 percent of GDP) that it is having to find ways to reduce inflows and increase *outflows*. Partly as a result of those capital inflows, the Chilean peso has remained remarkably stable in the year following the onset of the Mexican peso crisis—being only 2 percent down against the U.S. dollar by December 1995.[42]

Third, the capital markets have generally been impressed by the continued adherence of most Latin American governments to economic liberalization and adjustment, irrespective of Mexico's crisis and its negative impact on the short-term growth prospects of some other Latin American economies. There is some concern, however, that other emerging markets could misread the lessons here to curb their economic liberalization programs (the Venezuela scenario), even though the case for doing just the opposite is compelling.

On the one hand, the Mexican crisis serves as a stark warning to all policymakers in developing (and indeed developed) countries that the margin for perceived errors in economic policy management is now extremely limited. Foreign investors will be paying much closer attention than in the past to such indicators as exchange rates and fiscal regimes. In fact, their informal scrutiny will likely prove stricter than any formal conditions imposed by the IMF or the World Bank.

On the other hand, World Bank officials stress that the Mexican crisis is not an argument against the rigors of a market-based system. Rather, it is a wake-up call for the entire Latin American and Caribbean region. The crisis has shown policymakers and the public alike that there are urgent unfinished tasks, and that there is little room for complacency. A recent World Bank report emphasizes that a rapid deepening of the reform process is the only way to counter skepticism in the international capital markets. More specifically, the report calls for a "second phase" of reform, with the priorities being to raise domestic interest rates, encourage private investment in infrastructure, reform labor codes and educational systems, and make the lower levels of government more flexible and responsive.[43]

Other analysts have made further points. First, although Latin American nations should welcome capital inflows, their domestic savings are much more important to long-term growth. Second, they should attempt to regulate portfolio investment better, even if that requires some short-term inconvenience. And third, exchange rates must be sufficiently flexible to give governments the ability to take short-term corrective actions without the danger of damaging their credibility.[44]

Conclusions

Two main conclusions, one practical and one conceptual, can be drawn with regard to European perceptions of the Mexican peso crisis. On the practical side, EU policymakers have begun to draw broad lessons for the long term. As part of the ongoing debate over large-scale reform of the IMF and the World Bank, the EU may seek to ensure that those institutions pay greater attention to the EU's regional interests (in Eastern Europe and the Mediterranean), that is, more in line with the member states' share of the funds' voting capital. Also, the EU should increasingly exercise its potential for economic leadership, spurred in part by lessons drawn from the Mexican crisis. Indeed, the EU's ability to broker the July 1995 global agreement on financial services—without U.S. participation—demonstrates more than mere potential. One problem that has not been clearly articulated, however, is defining in whose "regional interests" the Mercosur countries fall, not to mention the rest of Latin America. The EU and the United States could well clash over such questions.

This possibility points to a second, more conceptual, conclusion. EU analysts believe that the Mexican crisis has demonstrated beyond a doubt the superiority of regional *integration schemes* (which Europe and Latin America favor) over mere *free-trade areas* (which the United States has advocated). At the heart of the matter is the EU view that it is dangerous to introduce freedoms of trade and capital movement in the absence of greater intrabloc economic and monetary cooperation and other counterbalancing measures, such as cohesion funds for the poorer regions. Free-trade areas simply do not encompass those kinds of measures. Manuel Marín, addressing the fifth EU–Rio Group summit in Paris on March 17, 1995, was clear in delineating the causal link between trade liberalization in the absence of significant cooperative arrangements and unhealthy financial speculation.[45]

It is true that the EU suffered tremendously from financial speculation in September 1992, when the lira and the pound were forced to diverge beyond the allowable European exchange rate mechanism (ERM) band and several other currencies had to be devalued. But there is consensus in Europe that, despite that battering, the ERM successfully prevented the speculation from having far worse effects. Under the ERM, the EU member states actively cooperated to stem the potential damage. Of further critical importance are the massive EU cohesion funds for the poorer member states, which have not only boosted economic development in the near term but also extended massive inflows of long-term capital.[46] Encompassing neither of those two mechanisms, NAFTA could not limit the extent or the duration of the financial and economic damage Mexico will have suffered by the time the peso crisis fully recedes.

In the wake of the Mexican crisis, and aside from its specific lessons for economic policy, the EU is becoming more aware of the potential scope for conflict with the United States. Not only are the two likely to clash over commercial strategies (questions of regional interests and market access), but they are growing farther apart in their respective views of the value of integration over mere free trade and capital movements. That divergence is most apparent in the EU's strategy for closer economic links with Latin America; although the EU is now pursuing accords on trade liberalization, it is primarily interested in establishing them with Latin American subregional entities rather than with individual countries.[47] Vitally, in both the commercial and the conceptual arenas, Europe seems to be more likely than the United States to be in tune with the needs and aspirations of Latin America.

Notes

1. Special thanks go to Peter Siderman for his substantial contribution to, and editing of, this chapter.

2. The Salinas administration had been reluctant to devalue the currency, particularly because doing so might damage the prospects of the ruling Institutional Revolutionary Party (PRI) in the elections of August 21, 1994. Upon taking office on December 1, 1994, President Ernesto Zedillo himself also ruled out a devaluation, ostensibly because he preferred a gradual and controlled erosion in value. A full analysis of the causes and wider repercussions of the crisis can be found in Institute for European–Latin American Relations (IRELA), "The Mexican Peso Crisis: National and Regional Implications," briefing paper no. 95/1 (Madrid: IRELA, January 30, 1995); and in IRELA, "Mexico: Economic and Political Shock," briefing paper no. 95/2 (Madrid: IRELA, March 22, 1995).

3. On average, those currencies lost 25 percent to 33 percent against the deutsche mark and other, stronger EU currencies during this period.

4. Moisés Naím, "Mexico's Larger Story," *Foreign Policy* 99 (summer 1995): 120.

5. Even some of the most recent analyses published in the United States have failed to capture the turnaround adequately, for example, Paul Krugman, "Emerging Market Blues," *Foreign Affairs* (July/August 1995): 43. The same applies to Moisés Naím, "Latin America the Morning After," *Foreign Affairs* (July/August 1995), particularly pp. 45–61, in which the author is pessimistic about the chances of resumed foreign capital inflows in the short term.

6. "Private Capital Flows to Third World Buoyant," *Financial Times,* January 24, 1996, p. 8.

7. Argentina was noticeably better placed than Mexico at the time: its current-account deficit was much smaller; its foreign exchange reserves were higher; its debt obligations were less concentrated in short-term instruments; and its political

and economic leadership was more stable (as demonstrated by President Menem's reelection four months later). See IRELA, "Argentina in the 1990s: Progress and Prospects Under the Menem Government," dossier no. 54 (Madrid: IRELA, June 1995).

8. Although some aspects of Brazilian economic policy resembled Mexico, Brazil enjoyed a series of advantages that meant it did not suffer to the same degree: Brazil had much higher currency reserves than Mexico and a far better trade balance (both in dollar terms and as a percentage of GDP) and was thus much less reliant on speculative capital flows. Brazil has in any case been far less dependent on the U.S. market. Nevertheless, the crisis has led to lower-than-expected capital inflows in 1995, making Brazil's (rising) trade deficit harder to finance. A detailed explanation of Brazilian economic policy and performance appears in IRELA, "Brazil Under Cardoso: Returning to the World Stage?" dossier no. 52 (Madrid: IRELA, January 1995), pp. 3–13.

9. OECD Survey on Mexico, issued on September 26, 1995.

10. "Mexico May Give Aid to 100 Companies: Debt and Tax Relief Planned," *Financial Times,* January 23, 1996, p. 6.

11. These are short-term dollar-denominated instruments that played a major part in the onset of the crisis. Only $6 billion of the $22 billion outstanding in January 1995 were still so in mid-1995. See *Economist*, August 5, 1995.

12. OECD Survey on Mexico, issued on September 26, 1995.

13. "Mexico: Unrealistic," *Latin American Economy and Business* (August 1995): 4–5.

14. Comisión Económica para América Latina (CEPAL), *Panorama económico de América Latina* (Santiago, Chile: CEPAL, September 1995), p. 17.

15. Shahid Javed Burki and Sebastian Edwards, *Latin America After Mexico: Quickening the Pace* (Washington D.C.: World Bank, June 1995), pp. 22–24.

16. "European Ire at Pressure over Mexico," *Financial Times*, February 5, 1995. Note that Robert Rubin's figure cited in Chapter 3 of this book refers to the IMF agreement to allow Mexico access to $7.58 billion *immediately,* with access to the remainder (up to $10.3 billion) to follow at an unspecified time. See "Mexico, the Long Haul," *Economist,* August 26, 1995, p. 17.

17. The loan effectively broke the fund's own rules. The World Bank and the Inter-American Development Bank also granted Mexico the biggest loans in their histories—on June 18 and 21, 1995, respectively—totaling $2.25 billion. EU observers doubt whether similar packages would have been available for Argentina or Brazil, for example, where European interests equal or outweigh those of the United States.

18. "El Grupo de los Siete logra superar sus diferencias sobre México en la reunión de Toronto," *El País*, February 5, 1995.

19. *Financial Times*, February 5, 1995.

20. "Mexico's Rescue," *Financial Times*, February 8, 1995; "Währungsfonds bewilligt Kredit für Mexiko—Rechtfertigung des Kraftakts durch IMF-Direktor Camdessus," *Neue Zürcher Zeitung*, February 4, 1995.

21. See, for example, "When Strength Is a Weakness," *Financial Times*, August 9, 1995.

22. "Feel-Good Factor Eludes U.S.: Import Anxieties Marred Labour Day," *Financial Times,* September 5, 1995, p. 7.

23. Naím, "Latin America the Morning After," p. 57.

24. Jeffrey E. Garten, "After the Uruguay Round: Competing to Win in the Global Marketplace," paper presented at the Council on Foreign Relations, New York, January 9, 1995.

25. Ibid.

26. IRELA, "Aid, Trade and Investment Flows: Distinct EU and US Strategies in Latin America?" briefing paper no. 4/95 (Madrid, IRELA: July 12, 1995), p. 2.

27. While in the 1990s the EU has tended to give more aid to Latin America than it has invested, U.S. FDI flows were seventeen times larger than aid flows by 1993, and this gap has continued to widen. The United States has been the main supplier of FDI in all the Latin American subregions, although EU flows have been strong to Central America (35 percent of the total) and to Mercosur (around 40 percent of the total). The EU position has been weakest in Mexico (11 percent), which receives half of all U.S. investment in Latin America. For a full analysis of the trends, see IRELA, "Aid, Trade and Investment Flows."

28. The Chilean foreign minister, José Miguel Insulza, noted on July 18, 1995, that Chile does not wish to participate either in the common market or in the common external tariff. Further, Chile seeks to remain outside the Mercosur institutions. An "association agreement" would thus chiefly involve better access to bilateral trade and investment. *Servicio de Información del Ministerio de Relaciones Exteriores de Chile*, July 19, 1995.

29. For more details, see IRELA, "Brazil Under Cardoso," pp. 31–32.

30. Such patterns indicate the existence of a "natural bloc" between the United States and the Greater Caribbean, in much the same way as between the EU and the Mediterranean countries.

31. In Mercosur's case, the EU will also provide support for the subregional integration process (on tariffs, technical assistance on regulating the internal market, and regional energy and transport projects). See IRELA, "XII EU–Latin America Inter-parliamentary Conference," base document (Madrid: IRELA, June 1995), p. 8.

32. Interview with Manuel Marín on July 11, 1995. Text issued by Directorate General for Audiovisual Information, Communication and Culture of the European Commission.

33. Officially referred to as a "contractual framework," this accord could involve an increase in EU humanitarian and food aid; technical assistance from the European Commission on institution building and structural reform; encouragement of activities by European nongovernmental organizations engaged in development and cultural activities; and some form of regular political dialogue between EU and Cuban officials.

34. *Agence Europe* (March 24, 1995): 8. The then prime minister of France, Edouard Balladur, had made a similar suggestion in an interview with *Notimex*, published in *Excélsior* on March 21, 1995.

35. Certainly, there are forums in which EU technical experts meet their Latin American counterparts (the EU–Rio High Level Economic and Commercial Meetings) or their ASEAN partners; and U.S. Commerce Department officials have met the Latin American trade ministers (as a result of the Miami summit) or Asian officials (at APEC meetings). But there is a need for the same types of routine contacts as those between the G-7 countries, at a much broader level.

36. The ACP countries are the non-EU member states of the Lomé Convention.

37. Naím, "Mexico's Larger Story," p. 128.

38. See IRELA, "Aid, Trade and Investment Flows."

39. "A Hazardous Helping Hand" and "G-7 Unity on Mexico Rescue Veils Discord on Tactics," *Financial Times*, February 6, 1995.

40. This trend goes far beyond Latin America. It is increasingly clear that foreign investors (particularly the large institutional investment funds) have discarded geographic factors in favor of economic policy fundamentals as a way of lumping

countries together. In this way, the Mexican crisis affected Turkey and Thailand (where policy developments have been similar to those in Mexico) at least as much as Brazil, and certainly more than Chile or Colombia. It is true, however, that in the earliest days of the crisis, U.S. investors' instinctive reaction was to reject all of Latin America.

41. To the surprise of many, Peru's stock market was, alongside Chile's, one of those least touched by the contagion effect. By the end of April 1995, both the Lima and Santiago stock markets had registered gains for the year. It is also notable that the Buenos Aires, Caracas, and Mexico City bourses were on a downward trend long *before* the contagion effect struck. See "Latin American Stock Markets," *Latin American Special Reports* (June 1995): 1.

42. "Emerging-Market Indicators," *Economist,* December 2, 1995.

43. Burki and Edwards, "Latin America After Mexico," pp. 1, 24.

44. Nora Lustig, "The Mexican Peso Crisis: The Foreseeable and the Surprise," *Brookings Discussion Papers in International Economics* (Washington, D.C.: Brookings Institution, June 1995), p. 23.

45. Manuel Marín, inaugural speech to EU–Rio Group Institutionalized Ministerial Meeting V, March 17–18, 1995, Paris.

46. Greece, Ireland, Portugal, and Spain. Ireland alone receives transfers of EU funds that are equivalent to 6 percent of its GDP. Even Spain, which has the largest share of cohesion funds but, relatively speaking, a much bigger economy, receives inflows equal to some 2 percent of its GDP.

47. This is why the EU was initially hopeful that Chile might consider joining Mercosur. The proposed accord with Mexico is a special case, being essentially a damage-control exercise after NAFTA. Even with respect to favorable General System of Preferences treatment, the EU has preferred to deal with the Andean group and a Central American group.

7

Lessons and Conclusions

Riordan Roett

As the essays in this book suggest, the Mexican peso devaluation of December 1994 was a "defining moment" for Mexico and for the emerging markets in Latin America. After a few years of heady expansion, in which "hot money" was drawn into the region's capital markets, rising U.S. interest rates and growing uncertainty about the stability of Mexico's macroeconomic future created a high level of investor anxiety in late 1994. The transition from the widely admired government of Carlos Salinas de Gortari to the "unplanned" presidency of Ernesto Zedillo on December 1 opened a period of "wait and see" on the part of the markets.

If, according to expectations, the new economic team, headed by Jaime Serra Puche, former trade minister and Mexico's negotiator of the North American Free Trade Agreement (NAFTA), continued the policies of Pedro Aspe, all would be well. Unfortunately, although Jaime Serra had been a superb trade negotiator, he failed to be as impressive a finance minister in his short tenure. Announcing the devaluation, almost furtively, Serra failed to consult with the investment community. After a short period of attempting "damage limitation," Serra was forced to resign, and Guillermo Ortiz, Aspe's former deputy, took over the finance ministry.

The precipitate devaluation decision created a classic balance-of-payments crisis. As Rogelio Ramírez de la O comments in his essay, following the devaluation "the market mounted a massive speculative attack against the peso . . . as it concluded that the government would lack sufficient understanding of market conditions and internal coordination to maintain it as promised." The Zedillo economic team proved itself unprepared—and perhaps naive—regarding the volatility and fickleness of the capital markets. Granted that there were serious flaws in the Salinas economic model, Ramírez concludes that the greater burden of responsibility rests with the inability of the Zedillo administration to understand basic market dynamics and external impressions of the strength—or weakness—of the Mexican peso.

113

While the macroeconomic stabilization and adjustment program of
1995 has produced significant current-account surpluses, and has allowed
the government to honor its *tesobono* obligations, it has impoverished millions of Mexicans. The banking system has been severely weakened and
the elements needed to stimulate a recovery remain controversial. The crisis has also raised important questions about the future of NAFTA and of
free-trade goals in the hemisphere.

The devaluation created what became known as the "tequila effect"—
a rapid spillover from Mexico to other emerging markets, principally in
the region. But as Albert Fishlow points out in the Foreword, in the end it
had little effect. This is, as he comments, one of the remarkable features of
the crisis, unlike similar incidents in the past where contamination was
widespread and extremely negative. Of particular concern in Latin America were the economies of Argentina and Brazil.

Roberto Bouzas, in discussing the reaction in the Argentine capital
markets, correctly indicates that crisis management became the hallmark
of Argentine economic policy in early 1995. The Menem administration,
led by minister of economics Domingo Cavallo, fought against the tide of
the contagion effect with appropriate policy measures and hard-sell public
relations. A new fiscal consolidation package was put forth in February, a
rapprochement with the IMF was negotiated, and the trade balance returned to a surplus position. Menem won an impressive electoral victory in
the presidential elections in May 1995, in large part due to the impression
that his administration knew what they were doing in responding to the
crisis created by the Mexican devaluation. The controversial Convertibility Plan, which was maintained even at high cost, ultimately helped maintain the government's credibility. Whether that will be so in the future is
open to discussion. But in the short term, the Argentine government reacted with alacrity and imagination to the peso crisis, which helped
dampen any contagion effect throughout the region.

After many years of economic misfortune and mismanagement, the
Real Plan in Brazil introduced widely admired stability in 1994–1995. A
new president, Fernando Henrique Cardoso, took office on January 1,
1995, as the crisis unfolded. He brought with him to the presidency a sea-
soned team of economic administrators who had served in the finance ministry and central bank in the prior administration and had worked closely
with him when he was finance minister. The new government opted for a
balance-of-payments equilibrium program, as Celso Martone points out in
his chapter. The first initiative was a devaluation in March 1995 and the
establishment of an exchange rate band. Interest rates were sharply increased. As these adjustments were undertaken, the Cardoso government
pursued its ambitious program of constitutional reforms. Early success re-
stored investor confidence in the largest regional economy; the surprising,
early success of Mercosur, the South American common market, also

helped. The Brazilian authorities were able to avoid the contagion effect because of the dynamism of the Brazilian economy and its general attractiveness to investors and the willingness of the new regime to devalue and continue with its reform agenda.

Redefining U.S.-Mexican Relations

While the escape from the contagion effect by major Latin American states is one of the most notable repercussions of the Mexican devaluation, the way in which the December crisis redefined U.S.-Mexican relations is another. As a result of the devaluation, the bilateral relationship between Mexico and the United States has become increasingly intense and multifaceted. Issues that had been ignored—or were ignorable—in the early 1990s have become prominent policy issues in the 1996 U.S. presidential campaign and in the Congress and the media.

Trade, immigration, and drugs have emerged as contentious policy questions along the Potomac and will not disappear in the foreseeable future. Drug policy has focused on the increased flows into the United States through Mexico and on whether the president should certify Mexico as a cooperative ally in the war on drugs. Trade policy emerged in the 1996 Republican primaries as a divisive topic. Moreover, with the apparent inability of the Clinton White House to win authorization for fast-track negotiations from the Republican Congress, the expansion of NAFTA is on hold and important steps in hemispheric trade integration have moved forward without the direct participation of North America. The 1995 financial support program for the Mexican economy, put together by the Clinton administration, remains controversial. The debate on immigration has turned negative as U.S. jobs are allegedly threatened by newcomers. And while the devaluation has had a major impact on the Mexican economy, it has not slowed regional integration as many thought it would. Interest has moved from NAFTA to South America and to the current dynamics in that region in which the European Union and investors have developed a new and healthy interest.[1]

The Drug Connection

As the Clinton administration struggled with the issue of "certification" in early 1996, federal narcotics officials, public interest groups, and members of Congress urged the president to decertify Mexico.[2] The recommendation was based on the flood of intelligence showing that Mexico had become a huge conduit for cocaine, methamphetamine, marijuana, and heroin sold in the United States. The issue was complicated by the delicate state of relations between Colombia and the United States. The Clinton

White House, in 1995, had decertified Colombia and then granted a waiver. In 1996, there was mounting pressure to completely decertify Colombia—and Mexico.

Mexican officials in Washington made it clear that they refused to recognize the legitimacy of the certification process and viewed it as an unjustified intrusion into Mexico's internal affairs. But granting certification, from the administration's viewpoint, was likely to create political repercussions with the Republicans as well as Democrats from those border states most impacted by the drug flows. And the administration was concerned over the impact of a decision to decertify on the political reform process in Mexico, the Zedillo government's efforts to manage its program of economic recovery, and the fate of NAFTA. A negative decision would also challenge the assertion of Zedillo that his government was making significant progress in the war on drugs. The stakes were raised in late February 1996, when Senator Bob Dole (R.-Kan.), the leading contender for the Republican presidential nomination, sent Clinton a letter urging him to certify that Mexico was not cooperating fully with the United States in the drug war.

On March 1, the White House announced that it had decided to decertify Colombia—without a waiver—and to certify Mexico. The immediate response on Capitol Hill was one of outrage. In a hearing before a House International Relations subcommittee on March 7, Republican representative E. Clay Shaw, Jr. (R.-Fla.) commented that "when you see that 65 to 70 percent of the cocaine coming into this country is coming in through Mexico or from Mexico, at that particular time it would make one wonder as to what extent the Mexican government is cooperating with us."[3] A movement in early 1996 to overturn the March 1 decision of the president had bipartisan support but, in the end, was unlikely to prevail. Congress has never overturned a presidential certification. But the proposed legislation reflected a deep strain of discontent among lawmakers who said that the administration had adopted an unjustifiably lenient approach toward Mexico and other countries. But the legislation, introduced in the House by Congressman Shaw, and in the Senate by Senator Alfonse D'Amato (R.-N.Y.), indicated the high profile of the war on drugs and indicated that it will continue to be one of the major policy items on the U.S. foreign policy agenda during the campaign and well thereafter.

Controversy over Trade Policy

For decades, the Republican Party saw itself as the party of "big business" and an unflinching defender of free trade. Suddenly, in the Republican primaries of early 1996, that position was shaken to its foundations by Patrick J. Buchanan. Using an anti–free trade, anti-immigration platform, Buchanan, the "spoiler" of the primary process, surged to early victories in Louisiana and New Hampshire. Building on the growing concern about unemployment and economic opportunity in "middle America," Buchanan railed against NAFTA and the new World Trade Organization (WTO). He attacked these agreements as a "sellout of American jobs, a sellout of American farmers, and a sellout of our sovereignty."[4] Throughout the early 1996 campaign, Buchanan pledged to pull the United States out of NAFTA and the WTO, the arbiter of trade rules around the globe. In a message that shocked the other Republican contenders, he proposed a 10 percent tariff on all Japanese goods, a 40 percent tariff on Chinese goods, and a high "social tariff" on imports from developing countries other than Chile.

As Buchanan dropped in the polls and Senator Dole secured the Republican Party nomination, the trade issue was not going to disappear. Economic nationalism had won a warm spot in the hearts of mainstream America. And the Buchanan message that free trade was bad trade was potent medicine to those who believed that their jobs were being exported overseas to Mexico and Asia. NAFTA emerged in the primary campaign as, at best, a mistake by the Washington establishment and, at worst, a deliberate effort at overlooking U.S. workers' interests in a fanciful commitment to fair trade in a world where there was little "fairness" due to government-managed trade strategies.

While the shift back to the center of the Republican Party would diminish the intensity of the debate about trade prior to the summer convention, the issue will not disappear. Trade-NAFTA-WTO-lost U.S. jobs is a new mantra in the United States and resonates strongly with the working class in both parties.

Immigration

Buchanan, in the primaries, often combined his recommendations on trade with a five-year ban on new immigration. The justification was simple. While one set of policies—free trade—was exporting jobs overseas, another set of policies—open immigration—was giving away U.S. jobs at home to low-wage foreign workers. Campaigning in Arizona in late February, the candidate stated the federal government had a constitutional obligation to defend the borders against "foreign invasion by Armies" and should also have that obligation for the thousands of illegal aliens he said cross the border every week. "Within six months, I'd stop illegal immigration across the border cold."[5]

In a pointed exchange with a young Mexican American in Phoenix at the end of that primary campaign, Buchanan acknowledged that Mexicans work hard "but they've got no right to break our laws and break into our country and go on welfare and some of them commit crimes."[6] And, in a campaign TV ad played in Arizona, Buchanan stated: "Each year, millions of illegal immigrants pour across our southern borders into the United States. Most come without job skills. Crime explodes. And who pays the cost of their health care, housing and welfare? You do. [I will] declare a 'time out' on new immigration, secure America's borders, and insist on one language, English, for all Americans."[7]

Again, with the falloff in Buchanan support in the 1996 primaries, the immigration issue will be less polarizing but it will not disappear. There is always immigration legislation pending in Congress. In early 1996, the Republican governor of California, Pete Wilson, an early dropout in the Republican primaries, sued the federal government for failing to reimburse his state for the costs of incarcerating undocumented aliens who have been convicted of felonies. State officials said that California, in 1996, had about 20,000 illegal aliens serving time in the state's prisons for committing felonies, at a cost of $400 million a year.[8] No matter the outcome of the lawsuit, the issue of immigration—legal and illegal—is an item of growing political controversy, and much of it is linked to the perception that the vast majority of the illegal immigrants originate in Mexico, driven by the lack of economic opportunity at home and creating escalating pressure on scarce jobs in the United States.

The Rescue Package

At the request of the Mexican government, the U.S. Treasury in early 1996 extended Mexico's access to the $20 billion support package through August. Senator D'Amato responded to that decision by introducing legislation to prevent any more extensions. D'Amato called the bailout a "failure" and said that the extension is throwing "good money after bad," and D'Amato's bill would block further extension of funds until Mexico takes steps to reduce drug flows. D'Amato and Senator Dianne Feinstein (D.-Calif.) want Mexico to comply with all outstanding U.S. extradition requests, to target and prosecute drug cartel leaders, and to pursue government graft and corruption cases. Seen as part of the ordinary politicking of an election year, the continued assault on the early 1995 rescue package, following the December 1994 devaluation, continued to create uncertainty about the capacity of the Clinton administration to hold the line against bipartisan opposition in an election year. A Republican victory in November 1996, and a Republican president in January 1997, would dramatically shift the terms of the debate and create a new source of bilateral tension between Mexico City and Washington, D.C.

The Reaction in the Hemisphere

For a brief time following the Summit of the Americas in Miami in December 1994, it was assumed across the hemisphere that Chile would quickly win accession as the fourth member of NAFTA. Other countries would then become logical candidates also. But with the devaluation of the Mexican peso in December 1994, and the inability of the Clinton administration to win fast-track authority from Congress, combined with the Buchanan assault on NAFTA, any expansion ideas were moribund in early 1995.

But the concept of regional integration continued to strengthen. Chile has proceeded to discuss an associate status with Mercosur—the South American common market composed of four members: Argentina, Brazil, Paraguay, and Uruguay. In early 1996, the European Union (EU) in Brussels and Mercosur signed a "framework" agreement to proceed with trade negotiations as well as a series of consultations on political and diplomatic issues. Chile is exploring a free-trade agreement with Canada. And the five countries of the Andean Pact—Peru, Bolivia, Colombia, Venezuela, and Ecuador—announced the creation of an Andean Community in March 1996. The decision was an ambitious attempt to revitalize their flagging twenty-seven-year-old trading bloc. The new organization, modeled on the European integration process, will be an effort to adapt the institution to the modern, free-trade world. Within five years, according to the Act of Trujillo, the 100 million plus inhabitants of the Andean Community will have a directly elected parliament and a genuine customs union. While both goals are ambitious—the EU-Mercosur arrangement in the Southern Cone and the resuscitation of the Andean Pact—they both indicate the deep commitment to regional trade integration with or without NAFTA's expansion.

While the Miami summit process continues with a series of multilateral consultations on technical areas of cooperation and concern, the dynamic has shifted, for the moment, to South America. Argentina's strong recovery from the "tequila" or contagion effect of the Mexican peso devaluation has strengthened its hand in Mercosur. Brazil's slow, often tedious, reform process is less spectacular, but it too defended its currency from the contagion effect early in 1995 and demonstrated an ability to avoid a costly devaluation and to set its own priorities. There was little impact on Chile of the devaluation in Mexico. The European Union, as Wolf Grabendorff points out in his chapter, supports a Latin American preference for regional integration schemes over mere free-trade areas, which the United States has traditionally advocated.

Final Conclusions

The aftermath of the December 1994 Mexican peso devaluation has not ended. But, unexpectedly, the principal reflection has been in U.S. domestic politics and in bilateral ties between the United States and Mexico. Elsewhere in the hemisphere, after a momentary sense of crisis, economic and financial developments have continued to deepen. Argentina and Brazil were forced to take defensive action after the devaluation, but their policy responses probably strengthened their economies in the long run. The European Union reaffirmed its commitment to working with regional trade initiatives in the Americas. And the regional blocs themselves, without abandoning the lofty goals of Miami, have proceeded to deepen the subregional integration process, which is more to their liking.

While NAFTA was the central piece of integration policy in 1994, since the devaluation the focus has shifted south. The ultimate return of NAFTA to a dynamic role in hemispheric integration will reflect the rapidity with which the Mexican economy recovers in 1996–1997, and U.S. skepticism can be overcome about the negative fallout from the agreement. And it will require a sorting out of the highly emotional issues raised in the 1996 presidential campaign regarding trade, drugs, and immigration— all of which have Mexico as a central focus of concern. The next U.S. administration—whether Democratic or Republican—will need to address the fallout from the bitter campaign debates and the ongoing concern in the United States about the efficacy of a strong and deeper relationship with Mexico when, in the minds of many U.S. citizens, it is the problem and not part of the solution for the economic prosperity of the United States in the twenty-first century.

Notes

1. "Argentina, Peru Presidents to Press for Trade Liberalization, Integration," *International Trade Reporter,* February 7, 1996.

2. Under a provision of the Foreign Assistance Act, the president is required to notify Congress by March 1 whether countries receiving U.S. aid are cooperating with antinarcotics policies. Countries deemed not to be fully in cooperation can be "decertified," making them ineligible for assistance; or they can be given a "national interest waiver" rather than outright decertification.

3. David Johnston, "U.S. Decision on Mexico Drugs Draws Opposition in Congress," *New York Times,* March 8, 1996, p. A2.

4. James Bennet, "Buchanan, Exalted, Pushes Economic Insecurity Theme," *New York Times,* February 22, 1996, p. A1.

5. Thomas B. Edsall and William Claiborne, "Rivals Hit Buchanan on Trade at Debate; Absent Dole Gets a Pass," *Washington Post,* February 23, 1996, p. A12.

6. Sue Anne Pressley, "Arizona Hails Dual Message of Buchanan," *Washington Post,* February 24, 1996, p. A10.

7. Thomas B. Edsall and William Claiborne, "Arizona Sits Atop Republican Divide," *Washington Post,* February 25, 1996, p. A10.

8. Steven A. Holmes, "California Governor Sues U.S. for Cost of Imprisoning Aliens," *New York Times,* March 6, 1996, p. A14.

About the Contributors

Roberto Bouzas is senior research fellow at the Latin American School of Social Sciences (FLACSO-Argentina) and the National Foreign Service Institute (ISEN). He is also an independent researcher at the National Council of Scientific and Technical Research (CONICET) and professor of international economics at the University of Buenos Aires.

Wolf Grabendorff is director of the Institute for European–Latin American Relations (IRELA) in Madrid.

Celso L. Martone is professor of economics at the University of São Paulo. He is also senior researcher at Fundaçao Instituto de Pesquisas Econômicas (FIPE/USP) and a member of the Fernand Braudel Institute of World Economics.

Rogelio Ramírez de la O is director of Economic Analysis for Company Planning (Ecanal, S.A. de C.V.) in Mexico City.

Riordan Roett is Sarita and Don Johnston Professor and director of the Latin American Studies program and the Program on U.S.-Mexico Relations at the Johns Hopkins Paul H. Nitze School of Advanced International Studies. He is also an adviser to the World Economic Forum in Davos.

Clint E. Smith is executive director of the North America Forum and consulting professor in Latin American studies at Stanford University. He is also a senior consultant on international and public policy programs to major U.S. foundations.

Index

Act of Trujillo, 119
Ajustabonos, 22
ALCAS. *See* South American Free
   Trade Area
Alfonsín, Raúl, 81
Alliance for Economic Recovery, 45
Andean Community, 119
Andean Pact, 101, 119
Anti-Inflation Pact, 17, 18, 22
Argentina: capital flight in, x;
   Convertibility Plan, 5, 6, 71–90, 114;
   crisis management in, 77–81;
   economic growth, 6, 76, 77, 96;
   economic policy, 114; elections in,
   ix, 80, 81, 87; exports, 21, 21*tab,* 75,
   76, 78*tab,* 84, 88, 92*n298;* gross
   domestic product, 6, 21, 21*tab,* 73,
   74*tab,* 78*tab,* 92*n26,* 96; imports, 73,
   76, 78*tab,* 84; inflation in, 5, 72, 74,
   75, 77; in international markets, 95,
   106; investment in, 73, 76, 77, 88,
   91*n11;* loss of reserves in, ix; *Pacto,*
   91*n8;* political parties in, 72, 82;
   privatization in, 73, 76, 81, 84, 85;
   productivity in, 20*tab;* public sector
   in, 73, 74, 74*tab,* 75, 76, 77, 81, 84,
   88, 92*n28;* reaction to peso crisis,
   5–7, 71–90; reform in, 6, 72, 78, 83;
   trade balance, 74*tab,* 76, 78*tab,* 82,
   84, 96, 114
Aspe, Pedro, 12, 13, 15, 16, 113
Assassinations, x, 15, 16, 47
Australia, 21

Balance-of-payments, 5, 19, 51, 61, 65,
   67

Bank for International Settlements, 35,
   39
Banks, 21; central, 4, 6, 15, 43, 51, 59,
   61, 71, 78, 79, 91*n12;* certificates of
   deposit in, 24; closures, 80, 83;
   commercial, 13, 14*tab,* 24, 28, 35,
   97; credit, 27, 28; credit portfolios,
   61; deposit insurance, 61, 80, 91*n14;*
   deposits in, 82–83; development, 28;
   Export-Import, 99; foreign
   borrowing by, 19; Inter-American
   Development Bank, 81, 91*n16,*
   110*n17;* international, 35; Japanese
   Export-Import Bank, 81; liquidity,
   19; losses, 97; mismanagement in,
   27; multilateral, 71; official, 53;
   overdue portfolios of, 28; panics in,
   61; private, 22, 45, 61, 80, 83;
   provincial, 80; reserves in, 71, 78;
   runs on, 71; weaknesses of, 9
Belgium, 96
Bentsen, Lloyd, 34
Bolivia, 101
Bonds, 94; "Argentine," 82, 84, 91*n17;*
   dollar-denominated, 9*n3,* 15, 95;
   Eurobonds, 24; global, 85; inflation-
   indexed, 22; peso-denominated, 15;
   redemption, 24; short-term, 9*n3,* 15,
   95
Bonior, David, 37, 40
Bouzas, Roberto, 6, 71–90, 114
Boxer, Barbara, 3, 36
Brady Plan, 34, 57
Brazil: Bresser Plan, 53; capital flight
   in, x; Collor Plans, 4, 53, 55;
   corruption in, 4; Cruzado Plan, 53;

debt in, 69*n4;* economic growth in, ix, 4; economic policy in, 49–68, 110*n8;* elections in, 57, 63; exports, 60*fig,* 66; gross domestic product, 4, 5, 52–53, 57, 59, 60, 61, 65, 68, 110*n8;* imports, 56, 59, 60*fig,* 62; industrial production, 61; inflation in, ix, 4, 49, 50, 51, 52–53, 53, 54, 54*fig,* 55, 60, 63, 65, 67, 69*n1;* in international markets, 95, 106; investment in, 52–53, 60, 66; liberalization in, 49; loss of reserves in, ix; modernization in, 55, 67; money supply in, 56*fig;* perspective on peso crisis, 49–68; political parties in, 5, 57; political system in, 54; private sector in, 57, 61, 63; privatization in, 5, 49, 53, 55, 56, 66; public sector in, 5, 49, 53, 55, 56–57, 65; reaction to peso crisis, 4–5; *Real* Plan, 49, 50, 53, 58, 60, 63, 64, 114; reform in, 50, 51, 53, 54, 55, 56, 59, 63, 64–67, 119; Summer Plan, 53; trade balance, 52–53, 58, 59, 60*fig,* 61, 110*n8;* Verão Plan, 53
Brazilian Social Democratic Party (PSDB), 5, 57, 58
Bresser Plan, 53
Buchanan, Patrick J., 116–117, 119
Bush, George, 34, 35

Camacho, Manuel, 45
Camdessus, Michel, 97
Canada, 21, 34, 35, 119
Capital: accounts, 19, 73; adequacy ratios, 79; cost of, 66; external, 77; flight, 6, 44, 61, 71; flows, x, xi, 6, 12, 15, 16, 18, 19, 27, 44, 52–53, 57, 58, 59, 65, 74, 76, 77, 78, 78*tab,* 84, 94, 95, 97, 105, 106, 107, 109, 110*n8;* foreign, 6, 12, 16, 18, 50, 58, 64, 69*n5,* 74, 76, 77, 78, 84; goods, 66; imports, ix; international, x; long-term, 109; markets, 5, 30, 52–53, 53, 56, 61, 67, 77, 84, 85, 87, 90, 94, 107, 113, 114; movements, 53, 68, 105, 108, 109; portfolio, 15; private, 30, 76, 85, 94–95; short-term, 27
Capitalism, global, 42
Cardoso, Fernando Henrique, 5, 57, 63, 64, 66, 67, 100, 114

Carpizo, Jorge, 15
Cetes, 15, 16
Chile, xi, 103; exports, 21, 21*tab;* gross domestic product, 21, 21*tab;* as investment-grade country, 107; membership in North American Free Trade Agreement, 47, 98, 118–119; productivity in, 20*tab*
China: exports, 21, 21*tab;* gross domestic product, 21, 21*tab;* productivity in, 20, 20*tab*
Christopher, Warren, 38
Clientelism, 63
Clinton, Bill, 3, 8, 9, 33, 34, 35, 38, 39, 41, 42, 43, 46, 92*n27,* 97, 100, 106, 115, 119
Collor de Mello, Fernando, 4, 55
Collor Plans, 4, 53, 55
Colombia: as investment-grade country, 107; relations with United States, 115–116
Colosio, Luis Donaldo, x, 15, 16
Common Agricultural Policy, 97
Convertibility Plan, 5, 6, 71–90
Corruption, 4, 46, 55
Credit: bank, 13, 27, 28; boom, 13; collateralized, 43; consumer, 13; contraction, 80; control of, 42; cycles, 4, 50, 52–53; domestic, 28; growth of, 42; lines of, 35, 36; policy, 65; restrictions, 61, 62, 68; rural, 69*n4;* squeeze, 61; subsidies, 61, 65; trade, 14*tab*
Crises: debt, 11, 26, 30, 52–53, 72, 77, 97; economic, 2, 31, 43; liquidity, 36
Cruzado Plan, 53
Cuba, 103
Currency: appreciation, 2, 13, 15, 19, 20, 27, 51, 76, 77, 89; board mechanism, 90; competitive, 14; control mechanism, 43; convertible, 6, 25, 71, 87; creation, 57; depreciation, 66, 89; devaluation, 7, 16, 17, 18, 19, 23, 24, 34, 36, 43, 46, 47, 50, 51, 61, 67, 68, 77–81, 93, 108, 109*n2,* 113, 114, 115, 119; domestic, 76, 77, 78, 79, 89; floating, 17, 46; foreign, 44; hard, 29, 97; management, 14–22; markets, 2; overvaluation, x, 14, 15, 16, 93; reform, 57; reserves, 110*n8;*

speculation, 14, 17, 22, 113;
   volatility, 97; weakening of, 28
Current-account, 6, 25*tab,* 61;
   adjustments to, 11; balances, 19, 84;
   deficits, x, 2, 5, 17, 18, 24, 50, 59,
   65, 68, 76, 78*tab,* 84; deterioration,
   76; external, 24; surpluses, 114

D'Amato, Alfonse, 43–44, 116, 118
Daschle, Thomas, 39, 40
Debt, 26; accumulation, 52–53;
   consumer, 60, 88; crises, 26, 30,
   52–53, 72, 77, 97; default on, 23;
   domestic, 16; external, 52–53, 72,
   81; floating, 77; foreign, 23, 26, 27,
   28, 34, 51, 52–53, 57; household, 95;
   interest, 25*tab;* private, 52; public
   sector, 24; reduction, 73, 91*n4;*
   renegotiation, 34; repayment, 28;
   restructuring, 84; rural, 69*n4*
Deflation, 90
Deregulation, 49, 73; economic, 18, 66;
   market, 55, 75, 89; trade, 102
Development: economic, 4, 42, 49, 67;
   neoliberal, 4, 49, 53, 62; social, 67;
   stabilization model, 4
Dole, Robert, 36, 37, 39, 116, 117
Drug trafficking, 43, 47, 115–116

Economic: adjustment, 23, 107;
   competitiveness, 18; crises, 31, 43;
   deregulation, 18, 30, 49, 66;
   development, 4, 67; growth, ix, 7,
   12, 15, 20, 72; infrastructure, 66;
   integration, 101, 108; liberalization,
   53, 95, 107; models, 18–23;
   nationalism, 117; policy, 2, 3, 5, 6,
   7, 34, 46, 49–68, 110*n8,* 114; reform,
   16, 17, 22, 30, 31, 43, 50, 63, 64–67,
   67, 72, 96; stability, 15, 50, 51,
   53, 72, 92*n21,* 103, 104, 106;
   stagnation, 54
Economic and Monetary Union, 97
Economy: "automatic adjustment" in,
   19; closed, 29, 31; competitive, 13,
   89; dollarization of, 79, 83;
   domestic, 19, 25, 27; open, 89
EFF. *See* Extended Fund Facility
   agreement
ESF. *See* Exchange Stabilization Fund
European Union, 119; Common
   Agricultural Policy, 97; Council of

Ministers, 102; Economic and
   Monetary Union, 97; European
   Commission, 102; exchange rate
   mechanism, 12, 108; exports, 99;
   Latin America strategy, 101–103;
   perspective on peso crisis, 7–8,
   93–109; reaction to rescue package,
   96, 105–106; relations with United
   States, 7, 96–97, 105–106, 109
Exchange rate(s): adjustments, 18, 63;
   appreciation, 13, 20, 30, 58, 59, 61;
   depreciation, 54*fig;* devaluation, 23;
   fixed, 18, 68, 72, 75, 79, 81, 82, 87,
   89, 95; flexible, 72, 108; floating, 2,
   45, 75; mechanism, 12, 108;
   nominal, 4, 13, 27, 30, 50, 51, 71,
   73, 77, 79, 81, 82, 87, 89;
   overvaluation, 19, 51, 65, 66, 68;
   pegged, 4, 18, 50, 51, 73; policy, 2,
   13, 17, 20, 24, 68, 86; real, 51,
   52–53, 59*fig,* 63, 74*tab,* 75; stability,
   12
Exchange Stabilization Fund (ESF), 3,
   8, 35, 39, 44
Export-Import Bank, 99
Export(s), 60*fig,* 76, 78*tab,* 92*n298,* 93,
   95, 97, 98, 99; growth, 19, 84, 88;
   manufacturing, 16, 38; profits, 14;
   stagnation, 66; taxes, 73; tax(es)
   rebates for, 75
Extended Fund Facility agreement
   (EFF), 76, 81, 85

Feinstein, Dianne, 118
Fishlow, Albert, ix–xi, 114
Foreign Assistance Act, 120*n2*
France, 104
Franco, Itamar, 5, 56
Free Trade of the Americas initiative
   (FTAA), 98, 100, 101
FTAA. *See* Free Trade of the Americas
   initiative

Garten, Jeffrey, 7, 99, 100, 106
Gephardt, Richard, 39, 40
Germany: exports, 21*tab;* gross
   domestic product, 21*tab;*
   productivity in, 20*tab;* reaction to
   rescue package, 96; views on
   intervention, 104
Gingrich, Newt, 36, 37, 39, 44
Grabendorff, Wolf, 7, 8, 93–109, 119

Gramm, Phil, 41
Greenspan, Alan, 37, 38–39, 97
Gross domestic product, 94; of
  Argentina, 73, 74*tab*, 78*tab*, 92*n26*,
  96; of Brazil, 52–53, 57, 59, 60, 61,
  65, 68, 110*n8*; of Mexico, 1, 4, 5, 6,
  12*tab*, 20, 24, 25*tab*, 46, 92*n26*, 93,
  96
Group of Seven, x, 9, 96, 104, 105, 106
Gurría, José Angel, 102

Helms, Jesse, 3, 37, 43
Hernández, Roberto, 16
Hong Kong, 21, 21*tab*
Hyperinflation, 55, 57, 72, 82, 92*n21*

Immigration, illegal, 37, 44, 47, 115,
  117–118
Import(s), 59, 60*fig*, 78*tab*, 84; capital,
  ix; increases in, 19, 76; protection,
  73; quota systems in, 62; reduced,
  18; restrictions, 62
Inflation, ix, x, 4, 5, 12, 13, 22, 24,
  25*tab*, 45, 47, 49, 50, 51, 52–53, 53,
  54, 55, 60, 65, 67, 69*n1*, 72, 73, 74,
  75, 77
Institutional Revolutionary Party (PRI),
  23, 31, 45, 109*n2*
Institutions: economic, 67; financial, 3,
  8, 85, 94, 96–97, 103, 104–105;
  international, 3, 8, 85, 94, 96–97,
  103, 104–105; multilateral, 80, 94,
  96–97, 106; political, 67; social, 9
Instituto Nacional de Estadísticas y
  Censos (Argentina), 96
Integration, regional, 8
Inter-American Development Bank, 81,
  91*n16*, 110*n17*
Interest rates, x, 5–6, 12, 13, 14, 22,
  26, 27, 28, 29, 47, 61, 62, 62*fig*, 65,
  66, 71, 76, 106, 113, 114
International Monetary Fund, x, 3, 9,
  16, 24, 25, 29, 30, 36, 39, 42, 44, 45,
  53, 71, 76, 80–81, 91*n10*, 94, 95,
  103, 106, 107, 110*n16*, 114
Interventionism, 63
Investment, 25*tab*, 88; direct, xi, 12*tab*,
  30, 66, 100, 104; domestic, 18, 44;
  foreign, xi, 12*tab*, 14, 15, 22, 25, 26,
  28, 30, 44, 66, 78, 100, 111*n40*;
  gross domestic, 73, 77; inhibition of,
  66; institutional, 91*n17*; portfolio,

28, 104, 107; private, 19, 29, 77;
  rates, 52–53–53, 74*tab*, 91*n11*; real,
  86; regulation of, 107; risks, 97
Italy, 21, 104; currency devaluation in,
  93; exports, 97

Japan: exports, 21*tab*; gross domestic
  product, 21*tab*; productivity in,
  20*tab*
Japanese Export-Import Bank, 81
Juppé, Alain, 102, 104

Korea: exports, 21*tab*; gross domestic
  product, 21*tab*; productivity in, 20,
  20*tab*

Labor: demand for, 90; markets, 22, 31,
  73; reform, 107
Lawson, Nigel, 18
Lending: collateralized, 43; commercial
  bank, 13, 14*tab*; for consumption,
  13, 14*tab*, 19, 21; for housing, 13,
  14*tab*; increased, 19; rates, 61
Liberal Front Party (Brazil), 58
Liberalization: economic, 49, 53, 95,
  107; financial, 53, 73; foreign
  exchange, 73; market, 30; trade, 4–5,
  6, 12, 55, 59, 76, 98, 99, 100, 103,
  106, 108
LIBOR. *See* London Interbank Offered
  Rates
London Interbank Offered Rates
  (LIBOR), 85

Malaysia, 21
Marín, Manuel, 102, 103, 108
Market(s): access to, 56, 84, 85; bond,
  95; capital, 5, 30, 50, 52–53, 53, 56,
  61, 67, 77, 84, 85, 87, 90, 94, 107,
  113, 114; commodity, 73;
  confidence, 15; consumer, 31;
  credibility, 16; currency, 2;
  deregulation, 55, 75, 89; domestic,
  61, 65, 75, 89; emerging, 5, 20, 42,
  53, 56, 97, 99, 100, 106, 114; export,
  43; financial, 15, 61, 65, 71, 73, 85;
  foreign exchange, 73, 97;
  globalization of, 104; international,
  5, 50, 52–53, 53, 56, 61, 65, 77, 85,
  87, 94, 106, 107; labor, 22, 31, 73;
  liberalization, 30; private, 84, 85;
  risks, 26; voluntary, 84

Martone, Celso L., 4, 49–68, 114
Menem, Carlos, 5, 6, 71, 72, 78, 80, 81, 82, 92n21, 114
Mercosur, 8, 62, 100, 101, 102, 103, 108, 111n27, 112n47, 114, 119
Mexican Bankers Association, 16
Mexican Debt Disclosure Act, 43, 44
Mexico: Alliance for Economic Recovery, 45; Anti-Inflation Pact, 17, 18, 22; austerity program in, 42, 45; Chiapas revolt, x, 11, 15, 34, 45; economic growth, 12, 12tab, 19, 20; economic policy, 34, 46; economic targets, 25tab; elections in, 31; exchange rate policy, 2; exports, 14, 16, 20, 21tab, 35, 93, 98; fiscal policy, 1–2, 15; flawed economic models, 18–23; gross domestic product, 1, 12tab, 20, 21tab, 24, 25, 25tab, 46, 92n26, 93, 96; illegal immigration from, 37, 44, 47, 115; imports, 93; inflation in, 1, 12, 13, 24, 25tab, 45; interest rates in, 14; in international markets, 95, 106; investment in, 14, 25tab, 30, 91n11, 104; monetary policy, 13; pactos, 46; policy errors in, 8; political parties in, 15, 23, 45, 109n2; privatization in, 3, 21; productivity in, 19, 20, 20tab; public sector in, 92n28; recession in, 26; reform in, 9, 14, 16, 17, 18, 20, 22, 29, 30, 31, 47, 96, 116; relations with United States, ix, 2, 24, 28–30, 115–118; savings in, 26; trade balance, 95

Nader, Ralph, 35
NAFTA. See North American Free Trade Agreement
National Action Party (PAN), 31
Neoliberalism, 4, 49, 53, 62
Netherlands, 96
North American Free Trade Agreement (NAFTA), 1, 3, 7, 8, 12, 15, 22, 30, 31, 33, 36, 37, 47, 93, 98, 99, 100, 109, 112n47, 113, 114, 115, 117, 119
Norway, 96

OECD. See Organization for Economic Cooperation and Development
Omnibus Trade Act, 99

Organization for Economic Cooperation and Development (OECD), 45
Ortiz, Guillermo, 2, 33, 39, 41, 42, 44, 45, 113

Pactos, 46, 91n8
PAN. See National Action Party
Perot, Ross, 34–35, 40
Peso crisis: Argentine perspective on, 5–7, 71–90; Brazilian interpretation of, 4–5, 49–68; consequences of, ix; contagion effect, 50, 60–64, 93, 96, 107, 112n41, 115, 119; European perspective, 7–8, 93–109; international perspectives on, 1–9; Mexican perspective on, 2–3; preventability of, 11–31; "tequila effect," ix, 79fig, 114, 119; U.S. response to, ix, 3–4, 33–47
Policy: credit, 65; domestic, ix, 27; economic, 2, 3, 5, 6, 7, 34, 46, 49–68, 110n8, 114; exchange rate, 2, 13, 17, 20, 24, 68, 86; fiscal, 1–2, 5, 27, 65, 68; foreign, 41, 100; industrial, 5, 62, 67; integration, 120; international, ix; macroeconomic, 2, 12–13; monetary, 13, 14, 15, 28, 65, 86; priorities, 27; reform, 92n21; regional, 100; regulatory, 83; stabilization, 30; supply-side, 76, 81; tax, 88; trade, 8, 51, 53
Political: assassinations, 34, 47; democracy, 33; participation, 31; parties, 5, 15, 31, 45, 57, 72, 82, 109n2; reform, 9, 31, 47, 116; stability, 38
Portugal: exports, 97; gross domestic product, 112n46
PRI. See Institutional Revolutionary Party
Price(s): adjustments, 57, 68; commodity, 84, 89; consumer, 63, 74tab, 75, 91n6; domestic, 4, 50, 63, 66; freezes, 49, 53, 55; increases, 24, 46; index, 63; international, 4, 50; movements, 57; nontradeable goods, 68; in privatization, 22; relative, 75, 89; stability, 51, 54, 60, 61, 65; tradeables, 75; wholesale, 75, 91n6
Private sector, 57; consumption decisions by, 19; foreign debt in, 27; investment, 19; liquidity crises in,

61; risk assumption by, 19; short-term bonds in, 24; spending in, 18–19; support for government, 16; wages in, 63

Privatization, 3, 5, 21, 22, 42, 45, 49, 53, 55, 56, 66, 73, 76, 81, 84, 85, 91*n4*, 95

Production, domestic, 66

Protectionism, 63

PSDB. *See* Brazilian Social Democratic Party

Public sector, 12*tab,* 53, 88; borrowing, 77, 88; debt in, 24, 65, 73; deficits in, 75, 76, 81, 91*n9;* discipline in, 90; divestitures, 74; foreign capital in, 84, 85; privatization in, 21, 49, 55; restructuring of, 29; revenues, 85; salaries in, 5, 81; wages in, 56–57, 65

Radical Civic Union (Argentina), 72

Ramírez, Rogelio, 2, 3, 11–31, 113

Real Plan, 49, 50, 53, 58, 60, 63, 64, 114

Recession, 6, 13, 26, 27, 29, 44, 51, 55, 57, 65, 68, 71, 82, 85, 89, 90

Reform: constitutional, 91*n8,* 114; currency, 57; economic, 16, 17, 22, 30, 31, 43, 50, 63, 64–67, 72, 96; fiscal, 53, 64, 66; institutional, 1, 5, 9, 67; labor, 107; legal, 9, 33; policy, 92*n21;* political, 9, 31, 47, 116; resistance to, 54; "second phase," 107; social, 9; structural, 4, 6, 14, 16, 18, 20, 22, 29, 49, 51, 53, 54, 55, 56, 59, 66, 72, 73; tax, 66; trade, 53, 56, 62

Resources: allocation, 77; in capital markets, 50; misallocation of, 13; supply of, 50

Rio Group, 104, 108

Roett, Riordan, 3, 4, 33–47, 113–120

Rubin, Robert, 34, 37, 38, 41, 44, 110*n16*

Ruiz Massieu, José Francisco, x, 15

Salinas de Gortari, Carlos, x, 2, 8, 13, 14, 16, 31, 34, 46, 93, 109*n2,* 113

Savings, x, 26; domestic, 46, 52–53, 53, 74; external, 77; investment, 74

Serra Puche, Jaime, 1, 2, 11, 17, 24, 33, 34, 113

Shaw, E. Clay, Jr., 116

Singapore: exports, 21*tab;* gross domestic product, 21*tab;* manufacturing investment, 21; productivity in, 20*tab;* savings rates, 21

Smith, Clint E., 1–9

Social: development, 67; infrastructure, 66; institutions, 9; reform, 9; security, 22, 46, 68, 76, 92*n20,* 92*n25;* tariffs, 117; tension, 26

South American Free Trade Area (ALCAS), 100, 101

Southern Cone Common Market, 100, 101

Spain, 21; currency devaluation in, 93; exports, 21*tab,* 97; gross domestic product, 21*tab,* 112*n46;* productivity in, 20*tab*

Stockman, Steve, 37

Summer Plan, 53

Summit of the Americas, 118

Switzerland, 96

Taiwan, 21*tab*

Tax(es): base, 81; codes, 75; collection, 5, 91*n7;* consumption, 85; distortive, 75, 89; export, 73; increases, 26, 81; indirect, 75; inflation, 26; local, 75; payroll, 88; policy, 88; rebates, 75; reform, 66; revenues, 65, 84, 87; social security, 92*n25;* structure, 88; value-added, 85, 91*n7,* 92*n19,* 92*n25*

"Tequila effect," ix, 79*fig,* 114, 119

Tesobono, 8, 9*n3,* 15, 16, 25, 28, 114

Thailand, 21

Trade: advocacy, 100; balances, 43, 52–53, 58, 59, 60*fig,* 61, 74*tab,* 76, 78*tab,* 82, 84, 95, 110*n8,* 114; barriers, 5, 35, 56; bilateral, 98; blocs, 105; deregulation, 102; flows, 97; foreign, 73; free, 5, 7, 62, 98, 100, 101, 104, 108, 109, 114, 116, 117; integration, 115; inter-American, 7; intraregional, 101; liberalization, 4–5, 6, 12, 55, 59, 76, 98, 100, 103, 106; policy, 8, 51, 53, 116–117; promotion, 4–5; reform, 53, 56, 62; regional. *See also* Free Trade of the Americas initiative

Turkey, 21

Unemployment, 9, 12, 13, 51, 65, 74, 74*tab,* 78*tab,* 82, 86, 87, 88, 95
United Kingdom, 18; currency devaluation in, 93; reaction to rescue package, 96; views on intervention, 104
United States: Contract with America, 37, 40; and European Union, 7; exports, 21*tab,* 38, 43, 98, 99; Federal Reserve System, 35, 97; Foreign Assistance Act, 120*n2;* foreign policy, 40–41; gross domestic product, 21*tab;* hemispheric strategies, 98–101; House Banking and Financial Services Committee, 38; interest rates in, 5–6, 71, 76, 113; investment in Latin America, 104, 111*n27;* "National Export Strategy," 100; national security interests, 44; Omnibus Trade Act, 99; opinions on North American Free Trade Agreement, 15, 35, 39–40; opposition to rescue package, 4, 36–46, 98; productivity in, 20*tab;* relations with European Union, 96–97, 105–106, 109; relations with Mexico, ix, 2, 24, 115–118; response to peso crisis, 1, 3–4, 28–30, 33–47; Senate Banking Committee, 44; Senate Foreign Relations Committee, 37, 38, 43; trade balance, 43; trade policy, 7, 8

Verão Plan, 53

Wage(s), 12; adjustments, 63; growth in, 14, 19, 20, 24, 46; minimum, 24, 25*tab,* 63; nominal, 68; public sector, 65; real, 13, 14*tab,* 24, 65, 74*tab;* stagnation, 65
Wilson, Pete, 118
World Bank, 29, 30, 42, 81, 91*n16,* 96, 103, 106, 107, 110*n17*
World Trade Organization (WTO), 102, 103, 117
WTO. *See* World Trade Organization

Zapatista National Liberation Army, 45
Zedillo Ponce de León, Ernesto, x, 1, 8, 9, 13, 16, 17, 18, 22, 34, 35, 44, 46, 95, 109*n2,* 113, 116

About the Book

The crash of Mexico's economy, triggered by the December 1994 devaluation of the peso, was felt well beyond the country's borders—from the Southern Cone in Latin America to the Potomac and Wall Street in the United States, and as far away as the European Union (EU) and the markets of Asia. This book analyzes key international policy issues that have been affected by the devaluation, from the perspectives of the United States, Mexico, Brazil, Argentina, and the EU.

Each author considers the policy implications of the crisis for a particular country or region, with an emphasis on the interplay between the economic effects of the devaluation and political and institutional changes under way—or delayed. A consistent theme in their chapters is the significance of developments in Mexico for other emerging markets.

Contributing to the book are Riordan Roett, Clint E. Smith (Stanford University), Rogelio Ramírez de la O (Ecanal, Mexico City), Celso L. Martone (University of São Paulo), Roberto Bouzas (FLACSO, Buenos Aires), and Wolf Grabendorff (IRELA, Madrid).

Riordan Roett is Sarita and Don Johnston Professor of Political Science and director of the Latin American Studies Program at the Nitze School of Advanced International Studies (SAIS), Johns Hopkins University. He is also the founding director of SAIS's Program on U.S.-Mexico Relations and Center of Brazilian Studies. He is author of numerous books and articles on Latin America and recently edited *Political and Economic Liberalization in Mexico* and *The Challenge of Institutional Reform in Mexico*.